Hirofumi Neda

I've never needed to visit doctors much, but since this series began, I've suffered from a whole heap of ailments, even though mostly all I do is sit around at home. Staying healthy is important, folks.

HIROFUMI NEDA began his professional career as a manga artist in 2007, winning the Akatsuka Prize Honorable Mention for his short story "Mom Is a Spy." After publishing several other short stories, he began working as an art assistant to Kohei Horikoshi on *Oumagadoki Zoo* and later on *My Hero Academia*.

KOHEI HORIKOSHI was born in Aichi, Japan, in 1986. He received a Tezuka Award Honorable Mention in 2006, and after publishing several short stories in *Akamaru Jump*, his first serialized work in *Weekly Shonen Jump* was *Oumagadoki Zoo* in 2010. *My Hero Academia* is his third series in *Weekly Shonen Jump*.

MY HERO ACADEMIA SMASH!!

VOLUME 2
SHONEN JUMP Manga Edition

STORY & ART BY HIROFUMI NEDA
ORIGINAL CONCEPT BY KOHEI HORIKOSHI

Translation/Caleb Cook
Touch-Up Art & Lettering/John Hunt
Designer/Julian [JR] Robinson
Editor/Hope Donovan

BOKU NO HERO ACADEMIA SMASH!!
© 2015 by Kohei Horikoshi, Hirofumi Neda
All rights reserved.
First published in Japan in 2015 by SHUEISHA Inc., Tokyo.
English translation rights arranged by SHUEISHA Inc.

The stories, characters and incidents mentioned in this publication
are entirely fictional.

Printed in the U.S.A.

Published by VIZ Media, LLC
P.O. Box 77010
San Francisco, CA 94107

10 9 8 7 6 5 4 3 2 1
First printing, November 2019

viz.com

shonenjump.com

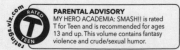

2

STORY & ART BY
HIROFUMI NEDA
ORIGINAL CONCEPT BY KOHEI HORIKOSHI

ALL MIGHT

The top hero whose very name rocks the world. He is also an incompetent newbie teacher.

IZUKU MIDORIYA

A hero fanboy who got his Quirk from All Might.

OCHACO URARAKA

Salt of the earth, woman of the people and a charming little scamp.

SHOTO TODOROKI

A troubled elite. Ridiculously good-looking.

KATSUKI BAKUGO

A child of the times whose dial is permanently set to "furious."

STORY

Izuku Midoriya has always idolized heroes—the people who use their Quirk powers to kick evil butt. A chance encounter with All Might gives him the Quirk he needs to attend U.A. High—an elite educational institution for heroes in training! Now, keep this on the down low, but Midoriya was actually stoked when his class got attacked by dastardly villains, since that meant he got to watch heroes in action, up close and personal.

MOMO
YAOYOROZU

TSUYU
ASUI

MINORU
MINETA

TENYA
IDA

FUMIKAGE
TOKOYAMI

KYOKA
JIRO

DENKI
KAMINARI

EIJIRO
KIRISHIMA

HANTA
SERO

MINA
ASHIDO

KOJI
KODA

TORU
HAGAKURE

SHOTA
AIZAWA

PRESENT
MIC

RECOVERY
GIRL

MT.
LADY

KAMUI
WOODS

MY HERO ACADEMIA SMASH!! 2

CONTENTS

COUP D'IDA

WOWEEE!

WHO KNEW THIS SPOT EXISTED ON SCHOOL GROUNDS?! *That's U.A. for ya.*

FULL BLOOM!!

TRAINING, THEY CALLED IT? MORE LIKE AN EXCUSE JUST TO COME HERE.

RIGHT?

COME NOW, EVERYONE!!

FWEEET!!

THERE ARE 94 CHERRY BLOSSOM TREES IN TOTAL!!

IT TAKES AN AVERAGE OF SEVEN SECONDS TO WALK FROM ONE TO THE NEXT, SO SHALL WE SPEND 51 SECONDS OBSERVING THE SPLENDOR OF EACH TREE?

HRM?! W-WHAT'S THE MEANING OF THIS?!

SORRY, PREZ, BUT YOU AIN'T GIVING ANY EXECUTIVE ORDERS! NOT TODAY!!

BAM **BAM** **BAM** **YANK** **BAM**

TODAY'S TRAINING CONCERNS JUST THAT, IN THE FORM OF PLANNING A SPRINGTIME PICNIC FOR VIEWING CHERRY BLOSSOMS!

HEROES MUST PROACTIVELY FIGURE OUT WHAT ROLE TO PLAY IN RESOLVING CRITICAL SCENARIOS.

NO. 21!!

JAPANESE CULTURE, WOOO!!

NAILING DOWN ROLES

I'LL BE IN CHARGE OF TAKING PICS!

I'LL CREATE WHATEVER ELSE WE NEED.

I CAN WHIP UP A GOOD WRESTLING RING FOR SUMO!!

POCKY GAME!!

POCKY GAME!!

YAY

WE'RE IN CHARGE OF GAMES!!

COME UP WITH GAMES THAT INVOLVE LESS KISSING, OR ELSE.

THOSE SPARKLES WON'T CONVINCE US.

Y-YOU BET.

DIFFERENT STROKES

PUT DOWN THE INSTRUCTION MANUAL FOR ONCE, DUDE.

IS THE GOAL NOT TO OBSERVE THE BEAUTIFUL BLOOMS, PER JAPANESE TRADITION?

LUNCH BOXES!! AND DANGO SNACKS!!

CHERRY BLOSSOMS MEAN IT'S TIME TO GET FRIENDLY WITH THE LADIES!!

SUMO WRESTLING UNDER THE FALLING PETALS!!

GRR!!

CAN WE SPLIT UP BY GENDER? THESE BOYS ARE OBNOXIOUS.

I SEE. WE'RE BEING TRAINED TO WORK TOGETHER, AND FAILING, SO FAR.

Vice President

P-PLEASE, EVERYONE, SETTLE DOWN.

YAP YAP

LET'S MAKE IT A SINGLES MIXER!

SUMO! YEAH!!

8

CAREER ADVICE

THEY'D BE IDIOTS IF THEY HADN'T.

IT SEEMS THE KIDS OF CLASS A HAVE FINALLY GOT THIS TEAMWORK THING DOWN.

IF YOU'VE GOT TIME FOR THAT NONSENSE, THEN YOU OUGHT TO START TEACHING FULL-TIME.

SINCE WE'RE HERE, HOW ABOUT IT, AIZAWA? A DRINK WITH ME, UNDER THE BLOS-SOMS...?

YOU KNOW HOW HE IS. DON'T TAKE IT PERSONALLY.

PORTABLE GENERATOR

I NEED A POWER OUTLET.

HRGH!! DO YOU MIND?!

THUNK

HERE WE GO.

QUIRK:
ELECTRIFI-CATION

HUH ?!

AW DARN, YOU'RE ALREADY USING THIS ONE?

NOT THERE !!

POKE

GUESS I'LL USE THIS ONE.

9

MASTER OF ALL TRADES

TEE HEE...

ALL THE SAME

RICE BALLS: SALT-FLAVOR

WE LEFT YOU IN CHARGE OF FOOD, AND YOU GIVE US THIS COUNTRY-BUMPKIN FARE?!

HUP HUP

FOOM FOOM FOOM FOOM

SHEESH. GIMME THOSE.

FWM FWM ZAM

TH-THIS IS HEAVENLY!!

BAKUGO'S A TOP CHEF TOO? WHO WROTE THIS CHARACTER?!

FW AP

GONE BUT NOT FORGOTTEN

THANKS, MAN!!

I'LL SAVE OUR SPOT HERE WITH THE TARP.

WHAT'S TAKING THEM SO LONG?

SHP SHP

?

DUN

OH NO!!

?!

ACK!! WE FORGOT ABOUT OJIRO!!

WHERE'D WE LEAVE THE TARP AGAIN?

AN ANT'S COME TO RUIN OUR PICNIC.

OUCH, MAN!!

FWP

HEY, HEY, YOU WERE GONNA HOLD A PARTY WITHOUT ME?!

BAM!

SEE?!

ET TU, PRINCIPAL?

REMEMBER, U.A. IS ALL ABOUT FREEDOM.

TAKE THE STICK OUT, AIZAWA.

I'M READY FOR THAT DRINK NOW.

YEESH...

YAP YAP

WE'LL ALWAYS HAVE...MEMORIES?

YOUTHFUL INDISCRETION

THIS HAPPENS ONCE A YEAR... SO YOU'VE GOT THREE CHANCES.

THE COUNTRY'S TOP HEROES SCOUT AT U.A.'S SPORTS FESTIVAL.

AND PREPARE AS BEST YOU CAN IN THE NEXT TWO WEEKS.

GRIT THOSE TEETH.

DEFINITELY POSSIBLE. BE ON THE LOOKOUT FOR ANYONE WHO LOOKS SUSPICIOUSLY OLD FOR HIGH SCHOOL.

I BET SOME KIDS TRY TO GET HELD BACK A YEAR ON PURPOSE, TO MAKE MORE ATTEMPTS.

ANOTHER HARSH STORY ARC?

WHADDAYA LOOKING AT ME FOR?! I'M THE SAME AGE AS YOU JERKS!!

UMM...

U.A.'S SPORTS FESTIVAL IS FAST APPROACH-ING!

WE'D BARELY LICKED OUR WOUNDS FROM THE VILLAIN ATTACK WHEN THE NEXT TRIAL WAS SET TO BEGIN!!

NO. 22!!

THAT'S *TOTALLY* ORDINARY !!

WITH ONLY TWO WEEKS UNTIL THE SPORTS FESTIVAL, WE'RE ALL GEARING UP TO TAKE THAT NEXT GIANT LEAP!!

EASIER WAY TO TELL THE WORLD

I NEED YOU TO TELL THE WORLD...

WHAT CAN I ACCOMPLISH IN THESE TWO WEEKS?! THINK, THINK!!

...."I AM HERE!"

I SHOULD GO FOR A JOG TO GET THOSE CREATIVE JUICES FLOWING!!

NO, THAT IDEA'S NO GOOD EITHER! ALL THIS THINKING'S BUSTING MY BRAIN!!

GRGH

TOSS

THAT BOY, I SWEAR. HE'S ALWAYS MAKING SUCH A MESS.

WHRRR

KSH

I AM HERE

OTHER KINDS OF INTELLIGENCE

HITOSHI SHINSO

FIRST-YEAR IN GENERAL STUDIES. INTIMIDATING!

DEPENDING ON THE RESULTS, THEY MIGHT CONSIDER TRANSFERS TO THE HERO COURSE.

BADUM

I UNDERSTAND THE REVERSE IS ALSO POSSIBLE FOR YOU...

REVERSE?

...?

UGH. HOW DID I LOSE TO THESE MORONS ON THE ENTRANCE EXAM?

WHAT HE SAID! WE'LL NEVER JOIN THE DARK SIDE!!

BAM

NO WAY WE'D BE TRANSFERRED TO THE VILLAIN COURSE!!

EAT THE RICH

FLOAT
FLOAT

I'D BETTER BULK UP.

I'M KINDA SCREWED IF IT COMES DOWN TO ONE-ON-ONES IN THE RING.

MAYBE PLEBS LIKE ME HAFTA GET BY LIFTING MILK JUGS AT HOME.

OH? URARAKA?

Get Swole with a Pro
2 hours for 12,000 Yen

2-Week Course
CHANGE YOUR LIFE
89,000 YEN

YEESH. WHO CAN AFFORD THIS CRAP?!

*$1,200 AND $890

MY FAMILY'S AGENCY HAS INVESTED IN THIS GYM, SO I CAN ASSURE YOU IT'S A QUALITY FACILITY!!

I-IDA?!

I DIDN'T REALIZE YOU FREQUENTED THIS GYM TOO!

MOM, DAD... NO WAY AM I LOSING TO MONEYBAGS MCGEE HERE!!

N-NAH, I'LL PASS.

WOULD YOU LIKE TO PURCHASE SOME STOCK? THEY REALLY ROLL OUT THE RED CARPET IF YOU DO.

D'OM

THE DANGERS OF CONTEMPLATION

MY ADMIRATION FOR MY BROTHER DROVE ME TO HEROISM.

I'M GONNA BE A HERO SO THAT MY MOM AND DAD CAN HAVE EASIER LIVES.

TMP
TMP

"THIS NEXT GIANT LEAP TOWARD BECOMING A HERO!!"

"IT'S ALL ABOUT AIMING FOR THE TOP."

"TIME IS LIMITED."

EVERYONE'S GOT THEIR OWN STRUGGLES. WHAT ABOUT ME?

HOW DID I GET HERE?!

WHERE AM I?

AH

WHAT THE HECK HAPPENED TO YOU?!

TWO WEEKS LATER

'SUP! I'VE SEEN SOME #@&$, AND I'M READY TO RUMBLE!!

BAM!!

IMAGINARIUM

GIVE US AN INTERVIEW, FUTURE NUMBER ONE HERO!!

CONGRATULATIONS TO OUR VERY, VERY TALL CHAMPION, MINETA!!

WAAAH

G CUP

*DELUSIONS OF GRANDEUR

MARRY ME, MINORU, YOU TOTAL HUNK!!

AMAZING!!

I HAD YOU PEGGED ALL WRONG!!

*THE POWER OF IMAGINATION

LINE UP, THERE'S PLENTY TO GO AROUND.

YOU'RE ACTUALLY THE COOLEST GUY AROUND!!

*TOTAL FANTASY

I DOUBT I COULD.

COULD I EVEN HANDLE SUCH A *BIG*, STRONG MAN?

YEAH, OKAY, I HAVE NO IDEA WHERE YOUR HEAD'S AT, BUT SLAM IT IN THE DOOR A FEW TIMES.

SORRY, JIRO, BUT I KNOW YOU CAN'T HANDLE *ALL THIS*...

SPARKLE

MODERN LINGUISTICS

THE MORE DATA SHE ACCUMULATES, THE MORE THINGS SHE CAN CREATE!!

KNOWLEDGE IS POWER FOR MOMO.

WAS SHE STUDYING CLASSICAL JAPANESE YESTERDAY OR // SOMETHING?

UH, SURE.

A THOUSAND BLESSINGS TO YOU ON THIS AUSPICIOUS DAY.

AND PORTUGUESE TODAY? HOW WOULD THAT EVEN HELP?

<OBRIGADA.>

YOU OKAY, YAOYOROZU?

LITERALLY CAN'T EVEN.

TOTES ME IRL!! DEF A BIG MOOD.

MOMO TAO?

CAN I REALLY USE MY QUIRK AGAINST PEOPLE?

TMP
TMP

TMP
TMP

BETTER FINE-TUNE THINGS...

DIP
DIP

AND I'VE ACTUALLY GOT AN ADVANTAGE UNDERWATER, SINCE LIQUIDS TRANSMIT SOUND WAVES BETTER.

I GUESS, THERE'S NO GUARANTEE THAT EVERY EVENT WILL INVOLVE RUNNING.

OH, JIRO! YOU'RE TRAINING OUT HERE TOO?

KAMINARI, YOU DOLT! STOP!!

KZZZT

I'LL TRY TO KNOCK OUT THE FISH, BUT NOTHING ELSE.

I OUGHT TO FINE-TUNE MY OUTPUT SO I DON'T OVERDO IT.

BADUM

EAR-PHONE JACK

FLOAT

OH NO, TSU-YUUU!!

LOOK!

FLOAT

OH NOOO, TSUYU?!

VISIBILITY

The scouts are sure to notice me now, oui? ☆

Well? It took me 13 hours to achieve this hairstyle.

SPARKLE

THERE'S NO POINT IN STANDING OUT UNLESS IT'S WITH YOUR QUIRK.

MORON.

MAYBE I SHOULD'VE DONE SOMETHING TO STAND OUT? GEL? OR WAX?

H-HAGA-KURE?!

HEY, GUYS!! WHO ELSE IS NERVOUS ABOUT THIS SPORTS FESTIVAL THING?!

MORNING!

ACTUALLY RELEVANT IN HER CASE...

I WASN'T SURE WHETHER TO PICK AN OUTFIT TO MAKE ME STAND OUT A LOT, A LITTLE OR NOT AT ALL.

THE DAY OF THE U.A. SPORTS FESTIVAL IS HERE.

NO, I AM HERE!

ALL OF JAPAN'S GOT ITS EYES ON US.

NO. 23!!

I NEED TO TELL THE WORLD THAT I AM HERE!!

18

FORBIDDEN SHIP

I NEED TO KNOW.

WHY DOES ALL MIGHT PAY SO MUCH ATTENTION TO MIDORIYA?

EAT LUNCH WITH ME, KID?

BREAK ROOM

SHLAK KLIK!

GLANCE

GLANCE

MAYBE I DON'T WANT TO KNOW.

NEVER MIND.

THE URARA STRUGGLE

I'VE GOT WRIST-BANDS TO HANDLE THE QUEASI-NESS.

A FINE WIND AT EIGHT KNOTS FROM THE WEST.

FWAP

FWAP

PRESS

ZERO GRAVITY

TIME REMAINING: 7 MIN., 32 SEC.

ZSH

I'LL ARRIVE JUST IN TIME !!

NOOO...

ZOOM

OH MY! I'M LATE, I'M LATE!!

WHY MEEE ?!

FSSSH

TIME REMAINING: 28 SEC.

WHAT FUELS YOU

DON'T GO DRINKING MY DRINK!!

SO SPICY!! WHAT IS THIS?!

FIVE-ALARM GINGER ALE

NOPE, I'M GOOD ...

WANT A SIP?

CONDENSED MILK

THAT'S, UM, NOT FOR DRINKING ...

THIS GREEN TEA'S A LITTLE WEAK, HUH?

IT'S MY POND WATER.

POND WATER

CAN'T BUY ME LOVE

Y'ALL ARE BEING DEPRESSING!!

NOPE. IT PAYS TOO WELL.

I COULDN'T TURN DOWN THIS SECURITY GIG.

THE KID FROM THE SLUDGE VILLAIN THING! HE GOT INTO U.A.?

HEY, THAT'S ...

WOW!! IT'S KAMUI WOODS AND DESTEGORO!! EVEN MT. LADY'S HERE!!

I'M SO HAPPY!! THANK YOU FOR YOUR AUTOGRAPHS!!

IT REMINDED THEM WHY THEY GOT INTO THIS LINE OF WORK.

THE THREE FOUND THE FANBOY'S SMILE MORE ENRICHING THAN THE MONEY.

EVERYONE'S PSYCHING THEMSELVES UP.

HMPH!

KRK

SLAP

NOT MAKING A BANNER FOR YOUR CLASS, AIZAWA?

Class B's homeroom teacher →

DESTROY CLASS A

I'M NO GOOD AT THAT STUFF.

?

BREATHE

YIKES, NOW I'M MORE NERVOUS THAN EVER.

MUTTER MUTTER

!

TMP

TMP

C'MON, GUYS! TIME TO GET THIS STARTED!!

YAOYOROZU? WHAT'RE YOU MAKING?!

ZRM

ZRM

CRE-ATION

FWIP

YOU CAN DO IT!! 1-A

PLUS ULTRA! 1-A

VICTORY OR DEATH!! 1-A

S-SAY WHAT?

OH, THESE? I'M JUST CLEARING MY MIND OF EARTHLY THOUGHTS.

TUNK

AIZAWA, YOU'RE SUCH A SWEETIE...

TWINGE

AWW...

SORE LOSER

NOW FOR THE ATHLETE'S OATH!!

KRAK!!

I, THE CLASS PRESIDENT, HAVE SPENT THE PAST TWO WEEKS PREPARING, AND PRACTICING THIS SPEECH!!

BADUM

MY TIME HAS COME!!

I'M READY!!

FROM CLASS 1-A, KATSUKI BAKUGO!!

YEAH, SOUNDED LIKE... SOMEONE WEARING GLASSES...

DID SOME OTHER KID JUST RESPOND?

PSST

PSST

PSST

PSST

STRESSFUL SYMPTOMS

THE FIRST-YEARS OF THE HERO COURSE... IT'S CLASS A!!

TRMBL

TRMBL

TREMBLING LIMBS

SWEATY PALMS

KASHINK

BOOM BOOM

STIFFENING UP

HUH? SHE WAS JUST HERE.

WHERE'D TSUYU GO?

GLANCE

GLANCE

INCREASED ANXIETY

PLAYING DEAD

DON'T CROAK ON US, TSUYU!!

WOMP!!

CHARACTER PROFILES!!

JUST LIKE IN THE LAST VOLUME, THESE PROFILE PAGES
ARE HERE TO POINT OUT HOW OUR BELOVED CHARACTERS
DIFFER FROM THEIR COUNTERPARTS IN
My Hero Academia PROPER!!
DON'T JUDGE TOO HARSHLY, OKAY?

RECOVERY GIRL

SHE'S THE NICE OLD LADY WHO SUPPORTS U.A. WITH
HER HEALING QUIRK.

WHAT EXACTLY DOES SHE DO TO TRIGGER THE HEALING
PROCESS? BASED ON EVERYONE'S REACTIONS, YOU'D THINK
IT'S SOMETHING OBSCENE!!

IN *SMASH!!*, SHE SEEMS TO HAVE BOUNDLESS ENERGY.
IT'S ALWAYS THRILLING WHEN YOU CATCH A GLIMPSE OF THE
HOT MAMA SHE USED TO BE.

ROBO-AIZAWA

THE FIRST BARRIER!

ROBO-AIZAWAS!!

BAM

EXPLAIN. NOW.

YANK

WHAT?!

THESE BATTLE-READY ANDROIDS ARE EQUIPPED WITH A.I. MODELED AFTER THE MAN HIMSELF...

YOWCH!! DON'T ASK ME!!

...WITH HARSH LECTURES!

YOU ALL FAIL.

ROBO-AIZAWA CAN'T ERASE QUIRKS, OF COURSE, BUT CAN STOP STUDENTS IN THEIR TRACKS...

WHRRRR

ALL OF CLASS 1-A WAS BROUGHT TO THEIR KNEES BY A SINGLE BOT!!

GLOOM

WHADDAYA KNOW!! IT'S SUPER-EFFECTIVE!!

HEY!!

THE FIRST EVENT OF THE SPORTS FESTIVAL...

...IS AN OBSTACLE COURSE RACE!!

THE REAL "OBSTACLE" WAS COMING UP WITH BLOOPERS FOR THIS!!

PLEASE FORGIVE ME.

NO. 24!!

24

WISH FULFILLMENT

THEY'RE REALLY STARTING TO MOVE!!

YAOYO-ROZU'S FELINE PLOY CREATED AN OPENING FOR CLASS 1-A!!

LOOKS LIKE FEWER ROBOTS TO DEAL WITH UP AHEAD?

WE COULD TRY THAT ON THE REAL AIZAWA.

MIND EXPLAINING YOURSELF?!

M-MIDNIGHT SENSEI?!

OUR REFEREE JOINED THE MIX?! AND STARTED ACTING OUT HER DARKEST FANTASIES BEFORE A LIVE TV AUDIENCE OF MILLIONS?!

HUH...? WHOA. I LOST MYSELF FOR A SECOND THERE.

WEAKNESS

I HEARD AIZAWA SENSEI LOVES CATS.

COULD YOU CREATE A CAT DOLL, YAOYOROZU?

YIKES, I WAS HOPING FOR SOMETHING CUTER AND LESS... ENCYCLO-PEDIC, BUT...

H-HOW DOES THIS LOOK?

AMAZING!! THIS IS A SIDE OF AIZAWA SENSEI WE'VE NEVER SEEN!!

WAIT, IT'S WORKING!!

I TOLD YOU, I DUNNO. SOMEONE IN THE SUPPORT COURSE?

WHO MADE THOSE ROBOTS?!

25

THE ENEMY WITHIN

I HAVE NO NEED TO WORRY! I HAVE ABSOLUTE FAITH IN MY SELF-CONTROL!!

VROOM

"We expected no less from you, President!"

"Yeah!"

I MUST EMPTY MY HEART AND FACE MYSELF!!

"You were this year's VIP, Ida!!"

"The king of cool, seriously!!"

"You're the champ of being awesome!!"

BEAM

OH NO, IDA LOST CONTROL!!

HRM?

CRASH

MIC'S LIFE, DANGLING BY A THREAD

THE FALL!!

THE SECOND BARRIER.

... WATCH OUT FOR THOSE SPECIALLY SELECTED DISTRACTIONS!!

TRMBL   TRMBL

PORN

IT MAY LOOK LIKE AN ORDINARY TIGHTROPE COURSE, BUT...

THE ENVELOPE WITH PICS OF THIRTEEN'S TRUE FACE IS A POPULAR ONE!!

IT'S ALL MIGHT'S DIARY FROM HIS TIME AT U.A.!!

Y-YUM, MOCHI.

ONE MORE STUNT AND YOU'RE DEAD.

I'M SO, SO SORRY.

PHOTO BOOK

WHAT'S THIS?! NOBODY'S GOING AFTER THE PHOTO COLLECTION OF ERASER HEAD'S ADORABLE SLEEPY-TIME FACE?!

MIND-FIELD

THIS DEADLY AFGHAN CARPET!!

THE FINAL BARRIER IS A MINE-FIELD!!

RUMBLE

THEIR SOUND BITES WILL TARGET YOUR DEEP-SEATED ISSUES AND REVEAL THEM TO THE WORLD!!

How, exactly?

MY HEAD?

SOME OF THESE MINES WILL TRY TO MESS WITH YOUR HEAD, SO WATCH OUT!!

KLIK

WHAT THE...?

I LOVE YOU, DADDY!!

BOOM

WHO CAME UP WITH THIS INSANITY?

NO, I COULD NEVER...

DOOM

WE'VE LOST SOMEONE ALREADY!! TODOROKI'S HEART JUST GOT SCOOPED OUT AND SERVED TO HIM ON A PLATTER!!

HER COMPLEX

LETTING THAT CRAP SLOW YOU DOWN? HAH!

LATER, YOU BUNCH OF LOSERS!!

BOM

BA M

INDEED.

1-A BADASS TRIO

AT THE VERY LEAST, I EXPECTED YAOYOROZU TO OVERCOME THIS CHALLENGE.

GLANCE

WERE THE GIRLS DEFEATED...?

R-REALLY, YAOYOROZU?

TRMBL

TRMBL

TRMBL

IDIOT'S GUIDE TO NOT BEING SOCIALLY AWKWARD

27

SELF-DESTRUCTION

K-KACCHAN?

DEKU IS ACTUALLY KINDA AWESOME...

TCH.

BOOM

U.A. IS WAY HARSHER THAN I THOUGHT IT'D BE...

SHADDUP!! SCREW THIS FREAKING MINEFIELD!!

SO WHAT IF IT IS?

FLASH

B-BAKUGO...

IT WOUNDS ME WHEN PEOPLE SUGGEST I'M NOT THE NICEST GUY...

I'LL GRIND YOU ALL INTO THE DIRT!! I'LL HAVE THE LAST LAUGH!!

KAZABOOM

THEY ALL DID SOME GROWING THAT DAY, BUT THE PSYCHOLOGICAL REVELATIONS WEREN'T USEFUL TO THE SCOUTS, SO THE KIDS HAD TO START OVER AND RUN A NORMAL RACE.

I'M WITH YOU, BAKUGO!!

NO, HE'S TOTALLY RIGHT!! NONE OF THIS CRAP MATTERS!!

RAAAAH

UNSHAKEN

F-CUPS!

I GAINED 2 KG!

FLASH

NOOOOO!!

BUGS ARE DELISH!!

DARK SHADOW IS ANNOYING SOMETIMES.

BOOM

WHO ON EARTH POSSESSES THIS HEART OF STEEL?

I WANNA TOUCH YAOYOROZU'S BOOBOROZUS!!

WHAT'S THIS?! ONE FIERCE COMPETITOR IS STROLLING RIGHT THROUGH THESE EXPLOSIVE CONFESSIONS?!

KABOOM

IN FACT, IT'S LIKE HE WANTS THE WORLD TO HEAR?!

YOU FLOAT MY ¤#*@#, URARAKA!

IT'S MINORU MINETA!! NOTHING SLOWS HIM DOWN!

FLASH!

CLASSIC URARAKA

BASEBALL WAS ONE SUCH CASUALTY.

THE ADVENT OF QUIRKS MEANT THE DOWNFALL OF MOST SPORTS.

I GOTCHA COVERED!!

I DUN GET THE RULES... WHOA, WHAT'S GOING ON, URARAKA?!

Loves baseball

BLAB

ME, PERSONALLY? I'M A FAN OF THE OLD WAYS. WHY, YOU ASK?

SO YOU'VE GOT OLD-SCHOOL BASEBALL, WITH NO QUIRKS ALLOWED, OR NEO-BASEBALL, WHERE QUIRKS ARE OKAY.

CUZ BASEBALL WAS ONE OF THOSE SPORTS THAT BROUGHT REAL STRATEGY INTO THE MIX.

BLAB BLAB BLAB

U.A. PARK

HAVE A SEAT, SONNY.

SHE'S LIKE SOME DRUNK GRANDPA TELLING US ABOUT THE GOOD OLD DAYS.

I SAID, SIT.

NAW, THAT'S OKAY.

THIS NEXT EVENT WAS *SUPPOSED* TO BE A CAVALRY BATTLE, BUT...

...WE'RE GOING WITH BASEBALL INSTEAD.

NO. 25!!

HUH?!

NOW IT'S A BASEBALL ARC.

HANDICAP	THE TELL

DIE!!

HARDEN-ING

MAKE IT FULL POWER, DUDE!!

I'M THE ONLY ONE WHO CAN TAKE BAKUGO'S PITCHES!!

RELAX, SON!! ALL YOU'VE GOTTA DO...

I'LL NEVER HIT ONE OF THOSE PITCHES!!

...STAND REAL STILL.

...IS JUST...

?!

HOW'D DEKU HIT THAT?

WALK!! GRR!!

WEE HEE HEE.

Strike zone

FOUR BALLS

THANKS FOR THE INFO!!

WHEN KIRISHIMA HARDENS UP, THAT MEANS A STRAIGHT PITCH IS COMING.

30

COACHACO	IDA THE HEEL

NAB

FROG

OUT!!

Right fielder

...BY RUNNING!!

SHP

SINCE QUIRKS ARE PERMITTED, THE BEST WAY TO MAKE USE OF MINE IS...

DARK SHADOW

NAB

OUT!!

NAB

DUPLI-ARMS

OUT!!

Left fielder

Center fielder

...THEN I SHOULD...

RM

IF MY ENTIRE OFFENSIVE STRATEGY CENTERS AROUND RUNNING...

RM RM

RM

URK

GRR

THREE OUTS! THAT'S THE INNING!

THEIR DEFENSE IS TOO GOOD!!

URK

VROOO!

BOP

...BUNT!!

GOOOO!!

WHAT SUPPORTIVE COACHING.

NEXT TIME, LET'S GO WITH SOME TRIED-AND-TRUE GROUNDERS.

HRMPH

CALM DOWN, SLUGGERS. WE'LL FIND THEIR WEAKNESSES YET.

YES, COACH!!

THAT WAS LAME!!

HMPH!! HOW DO YOU LIKE ME NOW?!

SKF

SAFE!!

WHO'S ON FIRST

FLOAT

O!!

WHIFF

EAT THISSS!!

ACK!

THAT'S STILL ON YOU, IDA!! GET THE BALL!!

He's running anyway!

H-HEY! THE BAT NEVER MADE CONTACT!!

BOOM
BOOM
BOOM
BOOM
BOOM

MOVE ASIDE, FIRST BASE TURD!! I'M HEADING ALL THE WAY HOME!!

GAAAAAAAHHHHHH?!

NOPE.

CRASH

SLIP

QUIRK (RIGHT SIDE): HALF-COLD

MAGICIAN OF THE MOUND

YEAH!!

RUSH

C'MON, YOU GOONS!! IT'S OUR TURN TO ATTACK!!

W-WHAT A WACKY PITCH!

WOBBLE

WHIFF

WHAP

STRIKE!!

ZERO GRAVITY MAKES FOR KILLER PITCHES.

CRUD!! I COULDN'T READ THAT ONE AT ALL!!

WHAT HAPPENED TO THAT HAPPY-GO-LUCKY GIRL WE KNOW AND LOVE?!

IS THAT REALLY URARAKA?!

GRIN

ATHLETE'S LAMENT

OUR FIRST BASEMAN'S CHILLY TRICKS...

...WON'T WORK ON HIM ANYMORE.

IT WAS LOOKING LIKE A SHUTOUT FOR TEAM BAKUGO, UNTIL...

...KATSUKI'S FASTBALLS SPED UP TO THE POINT WHERE NOBODY COULD HIT THEM...

BOOM

BOOM

BOOM

AND IF THEY TIE THIS UP AND THE GAME GOES INTO EXTRA INNINGS...

...THERE'S NO GUARANTEE WE CAN KEEP THE LEAD.

HUFF

HUFF

...AND BASE-STEALING QUEEN TORU HAGAKURE MADE IT HOME ENOUGH TIMES...

...TO BRING THEM WITHIN ONE RUN OF THEIR OPPONENT.

WHERE IS SHE?

EVERYTHING'S RIDING ON ME NOW.

I OVER-USED MY QUIRK, BUT I'VE STILL GOT ONE PITCH LEFT IN ME.

HUFF

HUFF

SO FOR THIS FINAL, FATEFUL PITCH...

...NO QUIRK.

HUFF

HUFF

FS~SH

AND BAKUGO...

...IS GONNA MAKE A RUN FOR IT, LEGAL OR NOT.

BOTTOM OF THE 9TH
7-6
OUTS: 2 STRIKES: 2 BALLS: 0

ZIP

KR AK

catch!

YOU **WANTED** HIM TO HIT THAT LAST ONE, HUH?

NICE, URA-RAKA!!

TAPE

RAAAH

GREAT PLAN!

THE TRICKSTER OF 1-A!!

WAY TO GO, COACH URARAKA! YOU MADE GREAT USE OF THE WHOLE TEAM'S QUIRKS!!

FINAL SCORE: 7-6
TEAM URARAKA WINS

THE DIAMOND AIN'T ABOUT FANCY, QUIRKY TRICKS.

WHEN'D I GO AND LOSE SIGHT OF WHAT MATTERS?

A HANDSOME CRACK. THAT.

NO!! IT WASN'T SUPPOSED TO END THIS WAY!

WAIT... WHAT ?!

HOORA!!

HOORA!!

END

...I FELL IN LOVE WITH.

THIS IS THE BASE-BALL...

34

FIERY BACK-AND-FORTH

QUIRK USE IS FINE TOO! JUST BE SAFE!!

ANYTHING GOES, SO LONG AS IT'S FUN!!

...BRAIN-STORM SHOW IDEAS!

ON THAT NOTE, LET US...

I GET TO SAVE DAMSELS IN DISTRESS!

THE HERO JUST OBLITER-ATES ALL THE VILLAINS, LIKE *BOOM!!*

ONE AT A TIME, PEOPLE!!

A BIG DANCE NUMBER AT THE END!!

BIG ACTION, UP ON A SKY-SCRAPER!!

A FORMER CEO TURNS TO VILLAINY WHEN HIS ENDEAVOR FAILS.

DEBATES ABOUT HEROIC EXPLOITS ALWAYS GET HEATED. NOT HEATED LIKE ENDEAVOR, TODOROKI!!

THE NOUN. NOT YOUR FATHER.

ENDEAVOR? UGH. BADUM.

NO. 26!!

IT'S GOLDEN WEEK IN JAPAN, AND SO IT'S TIME FOR A HERO SHOW EXTRAORDI-NAIRE!!

FROM PLANNING TO PERFOR-MANCE, THE KIDS OF 1-A ARE PUTTING ON A SPECTAC-ULAR SHOW AT A THEME PARK...

...AND THEY'RE EVEN GETTING ALL MIGHT'S ASSIS-TANCE!!

CLASS 1-A'S TRUE CALLING

...HAS COME WITH HIS GOONS TO PERPETRATE ALL SORTS OF ATROCITIES.

LORD EXPLOSION MURDER, THE BOSS BADDIE...

GRR!

BAM

AUDIO

LIGHTING

I'LL MURDER YOU ALL WITH EXPLOSIONS!!

BWOOM

PYRO-TECHNICS

LOOKS LIKE SOME TOP-TIER STAGECRAFT!!

TH-THIS SHOW'S ACTUALLY GONNA BE GOOD?

BADUM

BADUM

BADUM

CASTING CALL

DAY OF THE SHOW

IT'S PRACTICALLY METHOD ACTING FOR YOU.

HAR HAR HAR, SHUT THE HELL UP!!

GAH

WHY DO I GOTTA BE A VILLAIN?!

VILLAINS

I'VE NEVER ACTED BEFORE.

I'M S-SO NERVOUS.

DAMSEL

HERO

WIRES

SMOKE

APPLAUD

STAFF

STAFF

FSSH

WIND

VROOM

STAGE CREW

36

DOING THEIR OWN STUNTS

YOU FORGOT YOUR CUE? LEMME REMIND YOU, NERD!!

ENOUGH!!

BWOOM

DIE!!

BOOM!!

DUDE... WAIT!

WAH!

DARK SHADOW

THIS IS JUST PRETEND, MAN! FOLLOW THE SCRIPT!

YOU'RE STOPPING ME?

BAM

HARDEN-ING

YOU CAN FEEL THE TENSION!

THE VILLAINS HAD A FALLING OUT?!

OUTTA MY FREAKING WAY!!

THE ACTION'S SO REAL I ALMOST BELIEVE IT!!

DM DM DM DM DM

A STAR ISN'T BORN

BLUSSSH

HELP, UM, ME... I REQUIRE HELP.

BLUSSSH

Y-YOU WON'T GET AWAY... WITH THIS?

WORMP

T-TAKE THIS...

...

TRMBL

TRMBL

DID THE MAIN CAST SKIP REHEARSAL?

UM, SO...

SILENCE

ACT II TWIST

OH NO! THE SKY-SCRAPER'S COMING DOWN ON THE HERO?!

WOBBLE

AH!

HUH?! WHY'D LORD EXPLOSION MURDER SAVE THE HERO FROM CERTAIN DOOM?!

BW

WHAP

UMM...

LISTEN, DEKU...

FRET

DID HE SAY "PAR-ENT"?!

ERM, M-MY LINE! WHAT WAS IT?

DON'T TURN TO VILLAINY... JUST CUZ... THE PARENT COMPANY COLLAPSED...

THE CROWD'S READING TOO DEEP INTO THIS.

THERE'S GOT TO BE A BETTER WAY, DAD!!

RAAAAH

MEANING THE WIMPY HERO IS LORD EXPLOSION MURDER'S SON, AND THE FATHER ONLY STARTED COMMITTING CRIMES TO INSPIRE HIS SON TO STAND UP AND FIGHT FOR WHAT'S RIGHT?!

PICK A GENRE ALREADY

THAT TREE IS CLIMB-ING.

L-LOOK UP THERE.

YOU'RE RIGHT!!

I'LL USE THE CHAOS AS COVER TO GET THE DAMSEL MYSELF!!

HUFF

HUFF

BOOBOROZUS

TREE

BAKUGO'S LITTLE RAMPAGE RUINED THE SHOW ALREADY.

EEK! SORRY.

CLOUD

PLK

PLK

MINETA, WE'VE HAD ENOUGH OF YOUR PERVERTED TREE-TMEANT.

I DUNNO WHERE THE FANTASY ELEMENTS COME IN, BUT I'M LOVING THIS!!

ESPE-CIALLY THAT TREE!

NOW THE TREE AND THE CLOUD ARE DUKING IT OUT?

WHAT A TWIST!!

...THE FLEDGLING HERO WAS INSPIRED TO BECOME THE GREATEST HERO OF ALL TIME.

RAAAH

A-AND WITH THAT...

Umm...

WHAT NOW?

ALL THE STAGEHANDS CAME ON STAGE. EVEN THE TREE AND THE CLOUD...

TMP

TMP TMP

THE WHOLE CAST IS BOOGYING DOWN FOR THE CURTAIN CALL! I'VE NEVER SEEN A STAGE SHOW LIKE THIS!!

IT'S A DANCE NUMBER!!

STAFF

Kaminari

I WANNA DANCE TOO...

N-NO MORE... W-WHY COULDN'T WE HAVE JUST USED THE REGULAR OUTLET?

ZZT

ZZT

HUH? WHAT DO I DO?

SHUZU

BADUM

BADUM

WHAT NOW?

HOW'LL THIS TURN OUT?

SHOW ME THOSE PUNCHES YOU THREW AS A YOUNGSTER, WHILE PLAYING HERO.

SCRATCH

SHEESH. SCRATCH

GROW STRONG ENOUGH TO STAND AGAINST ME, MY FOOLISH SON.

POM POM

BEST DAD EVER!!

RAA HH

JUST ONE GOOD PUNCH WILL REACH MY HEART.

WHOA? TODO-ROKI?!

RAH

THE TALENTED MR. BAKUGO STRIKES AGAIN.

WHAT A TOUCH-ING STORY.

SNIFFLE

STAFF

VIRAL SUCCESS

IT FEELS LIKE WE ACTUALLY MANAGED TO ENTERTAIN THESE PEOPLE.

INCREDIBLE...

...SOMEHOW MADE IT EVEN MORE EXCITING.

CRAMMING EVERYONE'S DUMB IDEAS INTO THE SHOW...

A RECORDING OF THE SHOW ENDED UP GETTING OVER 100,000 VIEWS ON YO-TUBE.

C-CAN SOME-BODY LET ME DOWN?

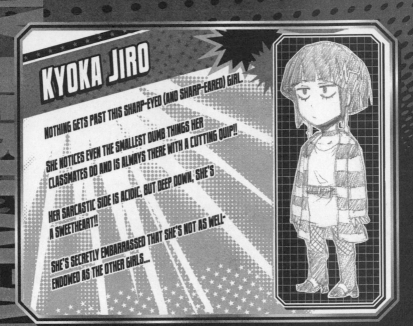

KYOKA JIRO

NOTHING GETS PAST THIS SHARP-EYED (AND SHARP-EARED) GIRL.

SHE NOTICES EVEN THE SMALLEST DUMB THINGS HER CLASSMATES DO AND IS ALWAYS THERE WITH A CUTTING QUIP!!

HER SARCASTIC SIDE IS ACIDIC, BUT DEEP DOWN, SHE'S A SWEETHEART!!

SHE'S SECRETLY EMBARRASSED THAT SHE'S NOT AS WELL-ENDOWED AS THE OTHER GIRLS...

SHOTO TODOROKI

MATURE BEYOND HIS YEARS, TODOROKI KEEPS A COOL HEAD WHILE DEALING WITH HIS FIERY FOOL OF A FATHER AND HIS MORE ANIMATED CLASSMATES.

HE SEEMS RESERVED, BUT INVITE HIM TO YOUR NEXT FUN EVENT AND HE'LL SHOW UP FIVE MINUTES EARLY, READY TO PITCH IN!!

SINCE HE GREW UP A SHELTERED ELITE, HE CAN COME OFF AS A LITTLE DETACHED, LIKE HE'S ALMOST TOO GOOD FOR THIS WORLD.

CLIQUEY

NO. NAP TIME.

SQUIRM

SQUIRM

BOO.

LET'S DO LUNCH, AIZAWA, OLD PAL!!

What shall we eat?

HEY, THIR-TEEN! WANNA GRAB SOME GRUB...

DO YOU GUYS WAN-NA...

Sounds good?

I want meat!!

HEY !!

"FIND YOUR OWN NAPPING CORNER !!

A SPORTS FESTIVAL MEANS EATING FRIED CHICKEN !!

AND RICE BALLS!! AND TAMAGO-YAKI!!

THE MAIN EVENT RESUMES IN ONE HOUR, BUT WE'RE GONNA FOCUS ON LUNCHTIME!!

NO. 27!!

KISS CAM MISS

SOMETHING ON YOUR CHEEK, MINETA MY DEAR.

OOH, I WONDER...

TEE HEE.

LICK THIS RICE RIGHT OFFA ME!!

FEEL FREE, MADAM FROG.

GAH! DON'T PUT IT ON THE JUMBO-TRON!!

HAHAHA

SEEMS LIKE ONE MEMBER OF CLASS 1-A STILL HAS TROUBLE FEEDING HIMSELF!!

REFLEXES

NAH. I BROUGHT LUNCH WITH ME.

LET'S GO BUY SOME LUNCH, BAKUGO.

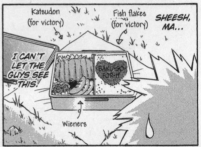

Katsudon (for victory)

Fish flakes (for victory)

SHEESH, MA...

I CAN'T LET THE GUYS SEE THIS!

Wieners

JOLT

SHF SHF

OH! THERE HE IS. BRING YOUR LUNCH THIS WAY, BRO.

TROUBLE IN PARADISE, YOU TWO?

OR NOT. WHAT-EVS.

UH... SORRY.

43

PENT-UP...MAYO

...

SO I'LL JUST HAVE A SALAD TODAY.

WOBBLE

I FEEL AS THOUGH I'VE BEEN PACKING ON WEIGHT LATELY.

I'M GONNA CHEW ON THESE AND FOOL MY TUMMY.

PUMP

S-SAME HERE.

WHY WOULD YOU DO SUCH A THING, JIRO?!

SQUIRT

ENJOY THOSE CALORIES.

MAYONNAISE

DOUBLE DISAPPOINTMENT

AHA! I'VE GOT A CHANCE TO SNEAK A PEEK AT SHOJI'S REAL FACE!!

SHF

ACK!!

QUIRK: DUPLI-ARMS

HE CAN REPLICATE HIS BODY PARTS AT THE ENDS OF THOSE TENTACLES!

BADUM
BADUM
BADUM

WHAT'S GOTTEN INTO URA-RAKA?

NOM

NOM

I THOUGHT SOMEONE WAS ACTUALLY INTERESTED IN ME FOR A SECOND.

MEH...

WHAT'S YOUR BEEF?

YOU KNOW, MY FATHER IS ENDEAVOR, THE NUMBER TWO HERO.

THE DINING HALL WILL BE PACKED IF WE DON'T HURRY...

!

THEN HE CREATED ME.

HE CHOSE TO MARRY MY MOTHER JUST TO HAVE AN HEIR WHO MIGHT BECOME NUMBER ONE.

HEY! I HEAR THEY'VE ONLY GOT FIFTY SERVINGS OF DELUXE WAGYU BEEF BOWL!!

YOU FOR REAL?! WE'D BETTER HURRY!

R-RIGHT, WELL...

AHEM. YOU WERE SAYING?

ACCESSIBILITY

THIS ISN'T THE BEST CHAIR FOR ME.

QUIRK: TAIL

BUT MAYBE I COULD SLIDE THROUGH THE GAP.

KLAT

OW!!

SQSH

IT'S CROWDED IN HERE, SO COULD WE USE THAT CHAIR?

PLOP

NOW BOTH MY TAIL AND MY NOODLES ARE LIMP.

SNIFFLE

ONE OF *THOSE* PARENTS

YES!!

SHOTOOOO!!

NO. 2 HERO: ENDEAVOR

GO, GO!! THAT'S THE SPIRIT!!

SHOTO!!

SHOTOOOO!!

RAWRRR!!

PIPE DOWN, FLAME-FACE.

WITH MY BLOOD IN THOSE VEINS, YOU'LL SURPASS EVEN ME!!

TODAY'S THE SPORTS FESTIVAL, RIGHT? JUST GIVE UP.

HE'S NOT PICKING UP.

AT ENDEAVOR'S AGENCY

NEVER MIND

BY RISING TO THE TOP WITHOUT USING MY LEFT SIDE, I'LL HAVE DENIED HIM EVERYTHING.

I HATE BEING NO MORE THAN A TOOL FOR THAT HUMAN GARBAGE.

EITHER WAY, I'LL RISE ABOVE YOU WITH JUST MY RIGHT SIDE.

YOUR CONNECTION WITH ALL MIGHT... KEEP IT TO YOURSELF IF YOU WANT.

I HEAR THEY FLEW IN TOP RAMEN CHEFS FROM ALL OVER THE COUNTRY TO MAKE US LUNCH!!

WHOA!! CAN'T MISS THAT!!

FOOD NOW, TALK LATER?

YEAH?

MIDORIYA...

YEAH.

FOLLOWING YOUR INSTINCTS

WELL, OF COURSE YOU'RE N—

I'M NOT ALL MIGHT.

AND TODOROKI...

...ISN'T YOU!

CAN I PLEASE GET YOUR AUTOGRAPH?

ALSO.

HE'S ALREADY THE NUMBER ONE FANBOY!!

BADUM

BADUM

SECRET SIDE

THERE YOU ARE.

SWP

E-ENDEAVOR?!

IN TERMS OF POWER, IT SEEMS ON PAR WITH ALL MIGHT'S.

I SAW WHAT YOU DID. THAT'S AN AMAZING QUIRK.

MY BOY, SHOTO, HE HAS A DUTY TO SURPASS ALL MIGHT...

TCH

I TOLD THOSE IDIOTS I WAS OFF WORK TODAY.

BEEP

RRRING

R-REALLY ENDEAVOR?!

HMPH...

!!

15:03

GLASS HOUSES

SHAKA SHAKA

FIDGET FIDGET

TWANNNG

TRMBL TWANG TWANG

TRMBL

OH? HOW ABOUT WE HAVE YOUR STUDENTS WRITE LOVE SONGS FOR THEIR CRUSHES?

CACKLE

POOR CLASS 1-A!! LOOKS LIKE THEY'RE LATE BLOOMERS, JUST LIKE THEIR TEACHER WAS!

NOPE, FAIR POINT!!

WE'RE STILL WORKING OUR WAY THROUGH THIS DANG SPORTS FESTIVAL!! BUT BEFORE THE FINAL EVENT...

NO. 28!!

AWW

...IT'S TIME FOR EVERYONE'S FAVORITE ACTIVITY!!

WHAT, YOU ASK? FOLK DANCING, OF COURSE!!

YEAHHH!!

48

RUDE AWAKENING

LET'S DANCE!!

HOWDY!

YOU'RE MY NEXT PARDNER, MIDORIYA!

DON'T HOLD ME SO TIGHT!!

SKWEEZ

HUG HUG

A-ASHIDO!!

OKAY, WHO'S NEXT?!

WAIT? WHAT DO I EVEN MEAN BY THAT? SHE'S HER OWN WOMAN, SO I CAN'T JUST GO PROJECTING AND ASSUME THAT SHE FEELS ABOUT THE WAY I FEEL ABOUT!

OUCH, MIDORIYA.

HANG ON, I'VE GOT URARAKA TO THINK ABOUT.

IT'S SUDDENLY SATO?!

YOU'RE CRUSHING MY HAND, THERE...

SKWEEZ

DANCING AMONG THE STARS

THIS IS KINDA AWKWARD, HUH?

WHOA!! I'M DANCING WITH URARAKA!!

ME? WITH URARAKA?!

BADUM BADUM

TOO COOL!!

...ON CLOUD NINE?!

I'M...

ZERO GRAVITY

FLOAT

FLOAT

SOMEBODY LASSO 'EM DOWN!!

THESE KIDS'RE HEADED FOR THE STRATOSPHERE!!

THE LEAPFROG JENKKA

CHA CHA CHA CHA
CHA CHA

CHA

?!

CHA CHA CHA CHA
CHA CHA

...

CHA

SORRY. NOT SURE WHY THAT KEEPS HAPPENING...

UNREQUITED

OUCH.

SORRY.

BOOM

OR IS IT BECAUSE IT'S WITH ME, SPECIFICALLY?

EVEN BAKUGO GETS NERVOUS DOING THIS SORTA THING?

BADUM

GYAHH?! WHAT'D I DO THIS TIME?!

BWOOM

BOM

OWW!

THOUGHT WE WERE GONNA GO STRAIGHT INTO THE TOURNAMENT.

SORRY... KINDA SWEATY FROM WARMING UP EARLIER.

50

SERENDIPITOUS

SAME.

FIDGET

FIDGET

I-I'VE NEVER DONE THIS BEFORE!

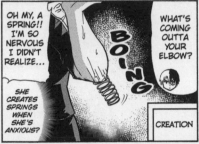

OH MY, A SPRING!! I'M SO NERVOUS I DIDN'T REALIZE...

SHE CREATES SPRINGS WHEN SHE'S ANXIOUS?

BOING

WHAT'S COMING OUTTA YOUR ELBOW?

CREATION

SORRY, I GOT NERVOUS TOO.

KRK KRK

SLIP

ACK ?!

HALF-COLD

WE'RE MADE FOR EACH OTHER...

BOING

BOYS' CLUB

SURE THING, BRAH! SHOW ME YOUR WORST!!

KINDA GLAD WE'VE GOT MORE BOYS THAN GIRLS. I SUCK AT DANCING.

OOF!!

WHAM

SPIN

SO SORRY!

I CAN TAKE ANOTHER ONE THOUGH!!

WINCE

HUH ?!

NOT A BAD HIT, BROJIRO...

BOYS ARE MORONS.

WHO'LL BE THE LAST MAN STANDING IN THIS FIGHT CLUB?

LEMME IN ON THE ACTION!

SHHH! FIRST RULE IS, DON'T TALK ABOUT IT!!

STANDARDS, PART 2

SHOULD A PRO HERO BE SO BITTER?

HMPH

YOUTH IS WASTED ON THOSE BRATS.

HAH!! NOT WITH YOU BUMS! I PREFER MEN WITH BRIGHT FUTURES AHEAD!!

CARE TO DANCE?

JOIN THE FUN, AUDIENCE MEMBERS !!

HA HA HA! HAVEN'T CUT A RUG LIKE THIS SINCE HIGH SCHOOL.

ALONE

IS THIS HOW THE STEPS GO?

OW.

SORRY.

A GIRL'S GOT PRIDE, BUT STILL!!

KA

HUH ?!

SLAM

WHY DO YOU BOYS GET TO HAVE ALL THE FUN?!

STANDARDS

I'M NEVER WASHING MY HANDS AFTER THIS!!

YE AA H

MY PRAYERS HAVE BEEN ANSWERED !!

SHE'S MORE YOUR SPEED.

NAH. NOT GONNA WORK OUT, SHRIMPO.

...

50 CM HEIGHT DIFFERENCE

WHY, FIFTY YEARS BACK, I STOLE HEARTS LEFT AND RIGHT.

C'MERE.

WORKS FOR MEEE !!

SWING

!!

WE MEET AGAIN.

IZUKU MIDORIYA
QUIRK: ONE FOR ALL

VS.

HITOSHI SHINSO
QUIRK: BRAINWASHING

STILL MORE SPORTS FESTIVAL!! WE'RE DOWN TO A SELECT GROUP OF COMPETITORS.

WHO THE HECK WAS THIS SIDE CHARACTER?!

UMM...

NO. 29!!

I'M THE WORST!! HE'S TOTALLY GONNA BE OFFENDED!!

URGH...

HE WAS KIND ENOUGH TO REMEMBER ME, YET...

WAIT? DID THAT BASEBALL GAME DETERMINE WHO'S FIGHTING NOW?

LET THE INEVITABLE SHONEN MANGA TOURNAMENT ARC BEGIN!!

NOT EVEN CLOSE!!

RIGHT, YOU'RE THE GUY FROM THE HERO MEET AND GREET WHO HAD ALL THOSE THEORIES ABOUT THE THING ATTACHED TO BACKDRAFT'S ARM!!

AHA

A BRIDGE TOO FAR

HE'S MOVING?! NO WAY!! BUT HOW?

GAH.

SNAP

STEP

SUPER-CONVENIENT QUIRK YOU GOT THERE!!

YOU'RE ONE BLESSED GUY! YOU KNOW THAT, RIGHT?!

DAMN! I JUST HAVE TO TRICK HIM AGAIN.

THE GIRLS IN YOUR CLASS TOLD ME YOU'RE A GROSS, STINKY POOPHEAD!!

STOMP

BUT THAT HAIRSTYLE? YEESH! AND TALK ABOUT NERDY!!

STOMP

WE SAID NO SUCH THING!!

FOCUS ON THE BATTLE, POOPHEAD!!

...?!

MASTER OF SELF-ESTEEM

-GOT HIM!!

GRIN

?!

SHK

QUIRK: BRAINWASHING

A FEARSOME POWER THAT LETS HIM CONTROL ANYONE WHO RESPONDS TO HIM VERBALLY.

WALK OUT OF THE RING.

JUST LEND AN EAR TO THE VOICES INSIDE YOUR HEAD!!

LIKE THIS!!

PULL IT TOGETHER, MIDORIYA! THIS IS WHEN SELF-CONTROL MATTERS MOST!!

WHERE'D THIS RUNNING GAG EVEN COME FROM?

HA HA!!

AMAZING IDA!

SEE...? I'M DOING IT RIGHT NOW...

THE CHALLENGE IS NOT BLUSHING!

JAPAN'S BEST!

54

WHAT'S WRONG, MINETA?

SHK

IZUKU MIDO-RIYA WINS!!

SLAM

N-need boobs.

N-not me. Body... moving on its own...

KRK

KRK

WISH I COULD JOIN THE HERO COURSE.

DARN.

RAH RAH

BODIES MOVING ON THEIR OWN, ETC.

NO, US TOO.

KRK

GAH, JUST KIDDING! DON'T HURT MEEE!!

FIGHT IT, EVERYONE!!

KRK

DID YOU COME TO LAUGH AT ME, CLASS 1-A CHICK?

I DIDN'T DO NOTHING!! YOU HERO COURSE NUTCASES ARE MESSED UP!!

HOW UNDERHANDED, YOU!! RELEASE THEM AT ONCE!!

YAP YAP

SAY WHAT ?!

AND FORCE ME TO BE A MORE CAPABLE PERSON?

NO, UM, I WAS WONDER-ING... COULD YOU BRAINWASH ME?

KIND HEART OF DARKNESS

IT WAS A POOR MATCHUP, SINCE TOKOYAMI IS POWERFUL IN ONE-ON-ONES.

YAOYOROZU WAS BEATEN IN AN INSTANT.

DO I NEED TO HURT YOU AGAIN?

H-HANG ON, DIDN'T HER CLOTHES GET ALL RIPPED DURING THAT LAST BIG ATTACK?

HE'S REPLACED HER RIPPED TOP WITH DARK SHADOW TO BLOCK PRYING EYES!!

WAIT, LOOK AT TOKOYAMI GO!! HOW CONSIDERATE!!

FWP

...FOR BEING THE LEAST BIRD-BRAINED BOY IN THE COMPETITION.

ON THAT DAY, TOKOYAMI GARNERED NATIONWIDE PRAISE...

RAYYYH

SHP

MOMOYAO'S SELF-WORTH

MOMO YAOYOROZU QUIRK: CREATION

VS.

FUMIKAGE TOKOYAMI QUIRK: DARK SHADOW

I WON'T HAVE THE LEEWAY TO HOLD BACK!!

I SEE THEY'VE PITTED ME AGAINST A TOP-CLASS OPPONENT.

ZRM

ZRM

TOP CLASS? HE RESPECTS ME THAT MUCH?

HRM...? ARE YOU FEELING UNWELL?

SHAKA

SHAKA

HE MUST'VE SAID SOMETHING BRUTAL TO YAOYOROZU!! SHE'S CRYING LIKE A BABY!!

WAAAH

Y-YAOYOROZU?

I'M SO HAPPY!!

FIRST DEATH IN THE SERIES

WHAT HAP-PENED?!

W...

NO WAY!! BRING IT ON, BUSTER!!

YOU GIVE UP?

KIRISHIMA IS NO MORE!! BAKUGO WINS!!

...FIVE MIN-UTES LATER

CRMBL

CRMBL

RECOVERY GIRL DID SOMETHING OR OTHER TO BRING HIM BACK.

W-WE'LL NEVER FORGET YOU, KIRI-SHIMA!!

LITTLE BY LITTLE

YOU AIN'T READY FOR ME.

I'VE BEEN WAITING FOR THIS, RIVAL!!

KATSUKI BAKUGO QUIRK: EXPLOSION

VS.

EIJIRO KIRISHIMA QUIRK: HARDENING

BOOOOM

HA HA HA!! THAT WON'T WORK ON ME!!

OH NO.

B B B BOM!

B

LOOK.

HE GOT CHIPPED AWAY INTO MINI-SHIMA!!

-ITTY-

BITTY!!

HEH! IS THAT ALL YOU'VE GOT?!

MOMO YAOYOROZU

SUPER CAPABLE X PANICKY + BAD LUCK = CRINGEWORTHY SCREWUPS

SHE GOT INTO JAPAN'S TOUGHEST SCHOOL ON SPECIAL RECOMMENDATION, WHICH MEANS SHE'S THE MOST CAPABLE STUDENT IN THE COUNTRY!!

DESPITE BLASTING AWAY THE COMPETITION IN AIZAWA'S QUIRK TESTS ON DAY 1, BAD LUCK SINCE THEN HAS REINFORCED HER ANXIETY. IT'S A VICIOUS CYCLE!

RECLAIM THAT THRONE YOU ONCE HELD, YAOYOROZU!!

MINORU MINETA

INCARNATION OF LIBIDO

HE GROPED ASUI'S CHEST, HE GOT AN UP-CLOSE-AND-PERSONAL VIEW OF YAOYOROZU'S BOOBOROZUS... THIS GOOD-FOR-NOTHING HAS GOTTEN AWAY WITH SO MUCH ALREADY!! HE DOES TRY TO KEEP UP WITH THE OTHER STUDENTS, AND HIS WEIRD QUIRK IS SURPRISINGLY VERSATILE, SO MINETA HAS GOT A LOT OF GROWTH POTENTIAL (PHYSICALLY AND MENTALLY)!! HOWEVER, HE'S TOO CALCULATING FOR HIS OWN GOOD, AND RUMOR HAS IT THAT HIS BEHAVIOR HAS LITERALLY STUNTED HIS GROWTH. IF ONLY HE COULD DIRECT SOME PERVY ENERGY INTO STUDYING... HE COULD DO A LOT IF HE ACTUALLY TRIED.

GATHERING INTEL

SHOTO TODOROKI
QUIRK:
HALF-COLD HALF-HOT

VS.

IZUKU MIDORIYA
QUIRK:
ONE FOR ALL

TODOROKI'S FIGHTS ALWAYS END IN A FLASH. I HAVEN'T LEARNED MUCH...

I'LL HAVE TO LEARN NOW. OBSERVE, AND LOOK FOR AN OPENING...

I'LL BE IN MY TRAILER.

DO YOUR THING!!

Action!

OKAY.

THE TOURNAMENT RAGES ON!!

NO. 30!!

MY HERO ACADEMIA TOOK 150 PAGES TO COVER THIS, BUT HOLD ON TO YOUR SOCKS, CUZ WE'RE GONNA DO IT IN FIVE!!

FIXED MATCH

I'LL SHOW MY FATHER...

...IS YOUR OWN!

YOUR POWER...

...THEN I DON'T REALLY THINK YOU'RE SERIOUS...

...ABOUT DENYING HIM EVERYTHING!

IF YOU BECOME NUMBER ONE WITHOUT GIVING IT YOUR ALL...

NNGH!

DID MY BASTARD OF A FATHER PAY YOU OFF OR SOMETHING?

YOU'RE PISSING ME OFF.

HAH! YOU ALMOST TRICKED ME INTO CHARACTER DEVELOPMENT!

NOT GONNA LIE...

UH, HE GAVE ME HIS AUTOGRAPH, YES.

EVEN A BROKEN CLOCK

MY LOBES HAVE FROZEN CLEAN OFF!!

FWOOSH

MIDORIYA VS. TODOROKI IS ONE CHILLY FIGHT!!

HUH?! WHAT'S THE CATCH?

TWITCH

SWF

GROSS!

W-WEAR THIS.

C'MON!! EVER HEARD OF GIFT HORSES AND MOUTHS?!

GRR!

AND HOW AM I SUPPOSED TO WEAR YOUR BABY-SIZED CLOTHES?

I AM FEELING A LITTLE WARMER.

THAT SAID...

Give it back then!!

TUG

PACING 101

...I HAVE TO END IT!!

I HAVE TEN SECONDS UNTIL MY ENGINES STALL, SO BEFORE THEN...

SHOTO TODOROKI QUIRK: HALF-COLD HALF-HOT

VS.

TENYA IDA QUIRK: ENGINE

THE FIGHT'S OVER IN TWO PANELS?!

HUHHH?!

SHK

TODOROKI WINS

I ONLY LASTED TWO SECONDS?!

HMM? I SEE ALL MIGHT DOING SIT-UPS.

CHECK OUT THAT CLOUD. LOOKS LIKE A NAKED LADY!

WAIT, THE CLOUD LOOKS LIKE DEEP-FREEZE IDA, ACTUALLY!

TCH! THANK YOU FOR KEEPING THE CONVERSATION RELEVANT!

TA-DA!

=

TOTAL RESEMBLANCE

ARE YOU TWO RESORTING TO IDLE PRATTLE JUST BECAUSE THERE'S EXTRA PANEL SPACE?

PLAYING WITH FIRE

IT'S NOT MY PROBLEM...

...HIS FIRE?!

FOOOM

HE USED...

...WHAT HAPPENS TO YOU NOW.

THANKS, MIDORIYA.

BUT...

WHAKOOOOOM

AW, CRUD!! HE AIN'T BREATHING!!

DON'T HEAD TOWARD THE LIGHT, MIDORIYA!!

GRD

SORRY, KID, BUT THAT OBVIOUSLY KILLED YOU!!

SEND ME BACK, GOD!!

DOTING DADDY

BEFORE THE FINAL MATCH

SNEAK

CHAK

PREP

STP STP

SHF SHF

!

LEAP

CHAK

I BETTER GO OUT THERE.

DO I HAVE A SECRET ADMIRER?

TEA AND A RICE BALL ...?

BING

MY NEIGHBOR DARK SHADOW

WHAT BLOOD-LUST ...

YOU'RE DEAD!!

FUMIKAGE TOKOYAMI
QUIRK: DARK SHADOW

VS.

KATSUKI BAKUGO
QUIRK: EXPLOSION

FLASH

STUN GRENADE!!

TOKOYAMI'S DARK SHADOW IS WEAK TO LIGHT!!

BOOM

SO YOU KNEW SOMEHOW...

BOOM

BOOM

POOF

AHH!! LOOK!! DARK SHADOW'S ALL PUNY AND WEAK NOW...

LIKE HE BELONGS IN AN OLD DECREPIT HOUSE IN THE COUNTRY-SIDE!!

CAREER APTITUDE

SORRY... I'M NOT SURE ANYMORE.

FINAL MATCH

USE YOUR FIRE ON ME TOO!!

C'MON!! USE THAT FIRE!!

I'M FEELING LOST...

THEN LEMME BEAT SOME SENSE INTO YOU!

I FREAKING SAID USE IT!!

YOU KNOW...

USE IT!!

I DUN- NO.

TODOROKI! DID NOT, IN FACT, USE HIS FIRE, SO BAKUGO WON THE TOURNAMENT.

NOPE.

...BAKUGO WOULD NOT BE SUITED TO CUSTOMER SERVICE.

MINETA IN THE MIDDLE

DUNNO. JUST FOUND THEM SITTING THERE.

YEAH?! GIVE 'EM HERE!!

GOOD LUCK, TODOROKI... OH?! GIFTS FROM A FAN?!

THE BARE MINIMUM I'LL SETTLE FOR IS TUNA- MAYO.

MUNCH

MUNCH

UGH. WHO BUYS PICKLED- PLUM RICE BALLS?!

PICKLED PLUM IS PERFECT FOR A QUICK STAMINA BOOST, YOU LITTLE DUNCE!!

BWAH ?!

EN- DEAVOR ?!

IT'S HARD TO FEEL SORRY FOR MINETA.

RAN INTO ONE PISSED-OFF ENDEAVOR IN THE HALL.

DID SOME- THING HAPPEN TO MINETA?

SHAKA

SHAKA

CRUCIAL TASKS

EVERY-ONE, STAND.

GO AHEAD, DAILY DUTY OFFI-CER.

BOW.

KLAT

C'MON... YOU'VE GOT SO MANY LITTLE JOBS ALREADY.

SHOULD THAT NOT BE A TASK FOR THE CLASS PRESI-DENT?

DIVISION OF LABOR, MAN!

SHAKA

SHAKA

NOT ANOTHER WORD, KAMINARI.

LET'S GET GOING, GUYS!

OUR NEXT BASIC TRAINING CLASS IS AT FIELD ALPHA.

FWEET

IDA NEEDS A TIME-OUT.

OH. I DIDN'T KNOW.

FUME

THE CLASS PRESIDENT OUGHT TO GUIDE THE CLASS TO ITS LESSONS!!

DID YOU GET ELECTED PRESIDENT? NO? THEN SIT DOWN!!

FUME

WITH THE SPORTS FESTIVAL OVER, THE KIDS OF CLASS 1-A GOT BACK TO THEIR (STILL-NOT-THAT) ORDINARY LIVES.

THIS IS MY HERO NAME.

DAILY DUTY: KAMINARI JIRO

DEKU

LET'S TAKE A LITTLE PEEK AT SOME OF THESE MORE MUNDANE MOMENTS!!

FOR INSTANCE, WHO'S GOT DAILY CLASSROOM DUTIES TODAY?!

NO. 31!!

64

AFFINITY

BOW-WOW?

B-B-BOW-WOW!!

S-STAND UP!!

S-SORRY.

KLAT

DAILY DUTY OFFICERS: MIDORIYA, YAOYOROZU

I-I HAVE TROUBLE WITH PUBLIC SPEAKING...

MIDORIYA, YOU NEEDN'T FEEL SO STRESSED ABOUT THIS.

"GIMME EVERYTHING YOU GOT!"

HMM? BUT MIDORIYA IS ALWAYS SO IMPRESSIVE...

UM, SPEAK FOR YOURSELF. THANKS.

THERE'S NOTHING QUITE SO TROUBLESOME AS AN INSECURE MIND.

HE'S JUST LIKE ME!

BEAM

WORRYWART

THAT'S ALL. GO HOME, FOLKS!

TOMORROW'S DAILY DUTY OFFICERS ARE MIDORIYA AND YAOYOROZU.

NOT YET. SENSEI HAS SOME ANNOUNCEMENTS.

SORRY, MOM, CAN YOU NOT TALK FOR A SEC?

MUTTER MUTTER

MUTTER

IZUKU, DID SOMETHING HAPPEN AT SCHOOL?

I KNEW ATTENDING U.A. WOULDN'T BE EASY FOR HIM, BUT I'M FEELING HIS STRESS VICARIOUSLY.

OKAY!!

HE LOOKS MORE TROUBLED THAN DURING THE ENTRANCE EXAM, THE VILLAIN ATTACK OR THE SPORTS FESTIVAL!

THAT'S SO ORDINARY.

OH

YES.

COULD YOU LISTEN TO ME PRACTICE MY DAILY DUTY OFFICER SPEECH FOR TOMORROW?

BOOK VS. COVER

WHAT ABOUT THE DAILY DUTY JOURNAL, BAKUGO?

LATER.

IT'S DONE.

WHEN DID HE...?

DONE!

!!

HE EVEN ADDED THE CLEANING NOTES!!

Cleaning Notes

SO MUCH DETAIL... HE'S UTTERLY METICULOUS.

BAM

WHAT A FUNNY GUY.

HEH

KATSUKI EARNED SOME BROWNIE POINTS FOR THAT ONE.

DUBBING, PART 3

FOR THE LAST TIME, YOU WON.

WE STILL NEED A GRUDGE MATCH TO SETTLE THINGS!

DAILY DUTY OFFICERS: TODOROKI, BAKUGO

EXCEPT I DID.

LIAR!!

STILL MOCKING ME, TWO-FACE?! I KNOW YOU DIDN'T FIGHT SERIOUSLY.

SHOVE

NO! I WOULD NEVER TOY WITH YOUR EMOTIONS ...

NOW KISS ME, YOU FOOL!

WAS IT ALL JUST A GAME TO YOU?!

FWP

WHO SAID THAT?! I'LL MURDER YOU DEAD!!

BOOM

| CANID | FWUFFY |

UM, ZERO AB-SENCES.

N–

DAILY DUTY OFFICERS: OJIRO, URARAKA

WHOA!

SEE YA, OJIRO.

OUTTA THE WAY!

AIZAWA SENSEI WILL BE...

NOW, ANNOUNCE-MENTS.

SHAKE.

FWP

HEY. OJIRO.

HUH?

H-HEY, URARAKA...

SHAKA

URARAKA, IS THAT A LEASH BEHIND YOUR BACK?

I SAID, SHAKE.

JUST TEN MORE SECONDS IN HEAVEN !!

QUIRK: TAIL

FWUF

FWUF

COULD I ASK YOU NOT TO TOUCH THAT?

TEACHER ENVY

BAM BAM BAM

IN YOUR SEATS NOW.

MUST BE NICE.

OOH!

SENSEI?

LOOK HERE!! CLASS B'S TEACHER LEAVES THEM ALL SORTS OF FEEDBACK IN THEIR JOURNAL!!

BUTT OF THE JOKE

GETTING GIRLS TO FAWN OVER YOU BY PLAYING UP THE PUPPY ANGLE?!

OJIRO!!

RRIP

OOPS. I'M STUCK.

AW, CUTE TAIL.

LEMME IN ON THAT ACTION!!

LOOK BUT DON'T TOUCH. OH, TOO LATE.

STUCK

OOF!

WHAP!

MOVE ASIDE, GRAPE-MISTAKE.

HRM?

NOOO!!

OWW... HUH?

STUCK

68

THE FROG STANDS ALONE

JUNE IS MY FAVORITE MONTH BECAUSE IT'S HUMID. RIBBIT

RIBBIT

I'M TSUYU ASUI.

WHO'S THAT GIRL WHO LOVES THE RAIN? IT'S... TSUYU!!

SAME!!

MY HAIR GETS ALL FRIZZY.

POOF

MY TAPE LOSES ITS STICKINESS.

YAAAY

ALL THESE ACCIDENTAL DISCHARGES... I'M EXHAUSTED...

DROOP

THE RAINY SEASON IS THE FROGGIN' WORST!!

TOADALLY!! WHO COULD EVER LOVE THIS WEATHER?

THAT'S RIGHT!! A WHOLE BUNCH OF LITTLE STORIES ABOUT TSUYU!!

LOSE WIN

THE BEST INTENTIONS

DON'T SWEAT IT.

S-SORRY, TSUYU! THIS IS YOUR FAVORITE SEASON, YEAH?

AW, YOU GUYS.

LET'S OPEN UP THE WINDOWS!!

I AGREE.

NAW, WE *SHOULD* BE SWEATING. THAT'S WHAT HUMIDITY DOES.

SAY GOODBYE TO THIS NASTY HUMID WEATHER !!

B AM!!

GOOD NEWS, EVERYONE!! I BORROWED THIS BIG OLD DEHUMIDIFIER FROM MY AGENCY!

HMM? WHY THE AWKWARD LOOKS, KIDS?

THE FROG SITS ALONE

I KNOW!! TODOROKI'S QUIRK COULD GET RID OF THIS NASTY HUMIDITY.

OKAY. SURE.

THE MOISTURE IN THE AIR WILL CONDENSE ON HIS COLD RIGHT ARM, ALMOST LIKE HE'S A DEHUMIDIFIER!

NICE!

REFRESHED

GOOD THINKING, MIDORIYA!!

70

HABUKO MONGOOSE

I'M HABUKO MONGOOSE.

SNAKE

YOU'RE ASUI'S *FRIEND*?!

FLIK FLIK

SO LITERAL.

LITERAL AGAIN?!

YEP, JUST LIKE THE JAPANESE IDIOM ABOUT SNAKES PARALYZING FROGS.

HER QUIRK LETS HER PARALYZE ANYONE SHE GLARES AT.

HMM. SEEMS DULL. STINKS LIKE NERDY FANBOY.

ANYWAY, THIS IS MY CLASS-MATE IZUKU MIDORIYA.

Hi there.

CAN I GET YOUR DIGITS, YOU AMAZING BADASS?

HISS

BUT I SAW THE WHOLE SPORTS FESTIVAL, AND YOU WERE SUPER-DUPER AWESOME OUT THERE.

F-FEELING COMPLIMENTED, BUT, STILL T-TERRIFIED!

SNAKES AND FROGS DON'T GET ALONG

OH, IT'S ASUI!!

RIBBIT RIBBIT

YIKES! A SNAKE?!

WHO'S THAT WITH HER? THE UNIFORM ISN'T FROM OUR SCHOOL...

DOOM

ASUI!! I CAN'T USE THE "DON'T CROAK" JOKE FOR A SECOND TIME!!

PLOP

NOT SO VENOMOUS

YOU'RE AN OLD FRIEND OF ASUI'S, AND YOU WANT TO THROW HER A BIRTHDAY PARTY?

OF COURSE WE WANNA HELP OUT!!

SPLENDID! I WILL HAPPILY PARTICIPATE!!

AREN'T YOU SUPPOSED TO BE SNOBBY ELITES?!

WHAT?! YOU FANCY U.A. KIDS ARE GONNA HELP ME?!

SHE'S A SWEETHEART. JUST NEEDS TO WORK ON HER DELIVERY...

HOW COULD YOU BE SUCH OBNOX-IOUSLY WONDER-FUL PEOPLE?!

SSSURPRISE

SHE'S HARD-ER TO READ THAN ASUI.

Y-YOU TOO.

...

GET HOME SAFE.

STARE

WHAT A WEIRDO.

THEY WERE FRIENDS IN MIDDLE SCHOOL?

BUZZ

A REQUEST?!

WHOA ?!

BADUM

BADUM

Haburn

Thx for hanging out.

I got a request, actually...

Could you...

...help plan the surprise party I wanna throw for Tsuyu's birthday?

!!

SHAKA

SHAKA

LET US ASK TODOROKI TO PRODUCE AN ICE SCULPTURE OF ASUI!!

AN ICE SCULPTURE?!

HOW ABOUT WE SING SONGS?

FIVE HOURS LATER

I'LL BRING HORNET LARVA AND GRILLED GRASSHOPPERS.

INDEED. WE WOULD REQUIRE SOME SORT OF CONFERENCE HALL.

ICE SCULPTURE

CAKE

LARVA

GRASSHOPPERS

PRESENTS

JAPANESE SAKE

LOCATION!!

WHERE THE HECK CAN WE HOLD SUCH A LARGE-SCALE EVENT?

A PUSHOVER WITH A LARGE HOUSE?

LOOM

HMM. WHO DO WE KNOW...?

THE HYDRANGEAS IN THE COURTYARD ARE IN FULL BLOOM!!

PLEASE COME!

SHE IMMEDIATELY AGREED.

YOU HAVE A COURT-YARD?

MERRY UNBIRTHDAY

HAPPY BIRTHDAY TO YOU...

HAPPY BIRTHDAY, DEAR TSUYU...

I'M TSUYU ASUI.

A LOT'S HAPPENED, AND I COULDN'T BE HAPPIER.

...TO HAVE SUCH GREAT FRIENDS.

I DON'T KNOW IF I DESERVE ...

...MY BIRTHDAY IS ACTUALLY FEBRUARY 12...

HAPPY BIRTHDAY TSUYU!!!

AND, WELL, NO SENSE IN GETTING HUNG UP ON THE DETAILS. ESPECIALLY SINCE...

NO PUNCH LINE, JUST AN EMOTIONAL PUNCH

THAT EAGER ABOUT THIS STUDY PARTY ...?

OH? YOU'RE ALL HERE ALREADY?

CHAK

T S U Y U !!

HAPPY BIRTHDAY

POP

HAPPY BIRTHDAY ...

TEE HEE... SURPRISED?

YOU'RE HERE, HABUKO ?!

WE LOVE YOU, TSUYU!

HAPPY BIRTHDAY! YOU'RE GREAT!

EIJIRO KIRISHIMA

VIRTUE, DUTY, HUMANITY, JUSTICE...
HE'S "MANLINESS" PERSONIFIED.

THIS ALL-AROUND GOOD DUDE IS ALWAYS CHEERY,
BUT HIS TENDENCY NOT TO SWEAT THE SMALL STUFF
MAKES HIM SOMETHING OF AN AIRHEAD.

STILL, THAT POSITIVE ATTITUDE OF HIS IS POSITIVELY INFECTIOUS!
KATSUKI LIKES TO PRETEND TO BE PISSED OFF BY THEIR FRIENDSHIP,
BECAUSE HE CAN'T ADMIT THAT KIRISHIMA IS LIKE CHICKEN
SOUP FOR HIS SOUL.

MIDNIGHT

SHOULD THE "R-RATED HERO" REALLY BE TEACHING ETHICS
CLASSES AT U.A.?

LIKE ANY HERO, SHE HOPES TO SAVE PEOPLE, BUT AT THE SAME
TIME, SHE'S CLEARLY GOT A FETISH FOR DANGER AND GENERAL
DISCORD. KINDA CART-BEFORE-HORSE.

IN FACT, THE REASON MIDNIGHT BECAME A HERO IN THE FIRST
PLACE WAS TO HAVE A FRONT-ROW SEAT TO ALL THE JUICY
DRAMA...

REALITY BITES!!

THESE DRAFT NUMBERS SHOW A CLEAR BIAS.

PICKED BY: 0   PICKED BY: 0   PICKED BY: 0

THE REST OF US ARE CHOPPED LIVER!!

BAKUGO GOT 3,000?! TODOROKI GOT 4,000?!

PICKED BY: 272

SO MANY OPTIONS. WHERE SHOULD I GO?

MAN, WHAT A QUANDARY.

THAT IDIOT HAS 272 CHOICES. I HAVE ZERO?!

BWUH?   TO HELL.

YOU WILL SOON BE STARTING YOUR INTERNSHIPS.

FOR THOSE WHO WEREN'T, THIS LIST HAS AGENCIES WILLING TO ACCEPT INTERNS. YOU CAN PICK FROM THERE.

THOSE WHO WERE DRAFTED WILL CHOOSE FROM THE LIST OF HEROES WHO SCOUTED YOU.

DEEPFAKE

THEY ONLY PICKED ME BECAUSE OF MY FAMOUS FATHER.

I'M NEVER GONNA LOSE TO YOU AGAIN, Y'HEAR ME?

PICKED BY: 4,123

PICKED BY: 3,556

OF COURSE IT DOES.

DOES NOT!

HUH?! 'SGOT NOTHING TO DO WITH YOUR DUMB DAD.

GRAB

I'M YOUR OPPONENT! LOOK AT *ME*!!

I KNOW THAT. YEESH.

DADDY THIS, DADDY THAT! YOU'RE ALWAYS BRINGING IT BACK TO HIM!!

STARE

THE WHOLE SCHOOL'S GONNA SEE THIS... AFTER SOME CREATIVE EDITING!!

I AM LOOKING RIGHT INTO YOUR EYES!

I SAID LOOK AT ME!! RIGHT IN THE EYES!

FIDGET

PICKED BY: 0

NUMBER THEORIES

IF WE'RE ZEROES, THEN THEY'RE ZEROES TOO! WE'RE BASICALLY UNBEAT-ABLE!!

SELF OTHERS
$0 \times x = ?$

IT'S NOT THAT BAD, GUYS!! NO MATTER HOW AWESOME THE TOP DRAFTEES SEEM...

PICKED BY: 0

UM. YEAH.

SPEAKING OF ZERO, THAT MAKES ZERO SENSE.

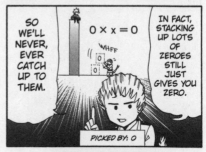

SO WE'LL NEVER, EVER CATCH UP TO THEM.

$0 \times x = 0$

WHFF

IN FACT, STACKING UP LOTS OF ZEROES STILL JUST GIVES YOU ZERO.

PICKED BY: 0

UGH. SORRY.

GLOOM

NOT HELPING, OJIRO.

PICKED BY: 0

PICKED BY: 0

PICKED BY: 0

ZERO LYFE

S-SERIOUSLY?!

SOMEONE HAS DRAFTED YOU!

ALL MIGHT'S TEACHER... I WONDER WHAT HE'S LIKE?

HE WAS MY HOMEROOM TEACHER.

HIS NAME IS GRAN TORINO.

NOT EVEN GONNA SAY GOODBYE TO YOUR OLD PALS?

HOLD IT, MIDORIYA.

I-I WAS IN A GANG?!

THE ZERO PROSPECTS CREW, YEAH!!

YOU WANNA LEAVE THIS GANG...? YOU GOTTA PAY THE PRICE...

YEAH YEAH

MORE 108 EARTHLY EVILS

DESPITE MY SHAMEFUL PERFORMANCE, 108 HERO AGENCIES SOMEHOW SAW POTENTIAL IN ME!!

108!!

Leggy Agency ("Lace Queen Hero") You've got the right assets to work with us.

G-Cup Woman ("Softcore Hero") That rack of yours? Basically counts as a Quirk on its own.

The Mayor ("Politician Hero") I'm in need of a new secretary.

CREATION

I HAVE NO CHOICE! THE SECULAR WORLD IS TOO CORRUPT!!

YOU'RE PREACHING TO THE CHOIR, BUT SLOW YOUR ROLL, MISSY!!

YOU WANT TO JOIN OUR NUNNERY? WAIT, DON'T CUT YOUR HAIR OFF RIGHT HERE!!

DELICIOUS DELUSION

...YOUR AWARENESS IS A MESS.

SO STIFF, AND...

PAT

PAT

WHOAAA!!

SO YOU END UP LIKE THIS.

HOPELESS

BUT NOT BECAUSE I LIKE STRONG GUYS OR ANYTHING! DUMMY!!

I'LL PREPARE US SOME DINNER NOW.

HOT 'N' COLD

BAM

YOU GOTTA FIND THAT ANSWER FOR YOURSELF.

THAT'D SURE BE NICE.

I'M HEADING OUT TO BUY SOME GRUB.

DESTROYED DELUSION

MUST BE A PRETTY OLD GUY.

ALL MIGHT'S TEACHER, HUH?

DAY 1 OF INTERN-SHIPS

SHABBY

HELLO? ANYONE HOME?

I'LL BE THE ONE TRAINING YOU IN GRAND-PA'S PLACE!!

MAYBE IT'LL BE A CUTE YOUNG GIRL INSTEAD? THAT'S A COMMON TROPE IN MANGA.

MUTTER MUTTER

WHO ARE YOU?!

WHAT'M I SAYING? I DIDN'T COME HERE TO HAVE FUN!!

GRAN TORINO

NOW SHOW ME WHAT YOU'VE GOT.

WHAT A GLOOMY YOUNG-STER.

FINE.

BLAH...

GAB

GAB

SO CLOSE, YET SO-BA

Y-YOU LIKE SOBA NOODLES, RIGHT?

ON PATROL

FIDGET

SHOTO TODOROKI
↓
ENDEAVOR'S AGENCY

FIDGET

YEAH.

FIDGET

FATHER AND SON

NO.

WANNA GET LUNCH THERE?

AHEM!

COME TO THINK OF IT, THERE'S A REAL FAMOUS SOBA SHOP JUST DOWN THIS STREET.

EXCELLENT! THAT'S EXACTLY THE LESSON I WAS TRYING TO TEACH!!

SLURP

THERE'S NO TIME FOR LEISURELY MEALS WHEN THERE'S PATROLLING TO DO.

EH?! WHAT ABOUT THIS LAVISH SPREAD?!

RESERVED

ENDEAVOR JUST CANCELED HIS LUNCH RESERVATION FOR TWO!

DON'T WORRY, I'LL HIT HIM WITH A HEFTY CANCELLATION FEE!!

NO. 34!!

THE YOUTHS OF CLASS 1-A NOW HEAD FORTH TO THEIR INTERNSHIPS AT PRO AGENCIES.

WHAT TRIALS DOTH AWAIT THEM DOWN YONDER PATH?! LET'S TAKE A LOOK!!

TRYHARD DAD

I'VE GOTTA REDEEM MYSELF TODAY.

YESTERDAY WAS A COMPLETE DISASTER.

LISTEN, FOLKS.

HE'S GETTING DESPERATE...

DON'T GO RESOLVING ANY YOUR-SELVES, OKAY?!

ARGHH!!!

SEND EVERY LAST INCIDENT MY WAY!!

I READ IN SOME BOOK THAT THIRD PARTIES ARE MORE CONVINCING.

ALSO, FIND TIME TO TELL MY SON ABOUT ALL MY ACCOMPLISHMENTS.

I SHOULD'VE TAKEN LONGER WALKING OVER.

THAT'S ALL! BACK TO YOUR DESKS BEFORE SHOTO GETS HERE!!

ROLE MODEL

MY BOY IS WATCHING ME CLOSE TO SEE HOW I GET THE JOB DONE!!

LOOK

I GOTTA DO SOME-THING HEROIC!!

GLANCE

ARE THERE ANY CRIMES THAT NEED FOILING?!

GLANCE

WHOA!

GLANCE GLANCE

TRIP

S-SIR?! WATCH OUT!

YIKES. BETTER NOT LET ANY OPEN FLAMES NEAR THAT MANHOLE.

BAD NEWS. THERE'S A HUGE GAS LEAK DOWN THERE.

LET THIS BE A LESSON!!

BURN

BURN

S-SURE.

DO I WANT TO KNOW?

GIVE AND TAKE

YES, MA'AM!!

CARRY THESE SHOPPING BAGS, MINETA.

GWAH!!

SQUISH

OOPS. AHH!

EVACUATE THE AREA, QUICK!

WORKING FOR A PRO HERO IS EXHAUSTING.

GUHH...

Stat!

Get me lunch!

...I CAN FIND THE STRENGTH TO KEEP GETTING BACK UP!!

BOP

BOP

DROPPED MY ERASER.

BUT AS LONG AS I'M PRIVY TO THESE BOOTIFUL SIGHTS...

COGNITIVE DISSONANCE

MINORU MINETA, AGE 15. CURRENTLY ACCEPTING GIRLFRIEND APPLICATIONS!

SHWP

SHWP

MINORU MINETA ↓ MT. LADY'S AGENCY

I'M SORRY!

YOU SERIOUS ABOUT BEING A HERO OR NOT?

MT. LADY'S ACTUALLY SCARY?!

ENOUGH OF THAT NONSENSE.

SMAK

BOING

SLSH

U.A.'S CLEARLY BEEN LOWERING ITS STANDARDS, HUH?

SHE'S SCARY, BUT I'M OKAY WITH THAT!!

YES. I AM A SNIVELING, WORTHLESS WORM.

...ANSWERED THE BOY, WITH A SMILE ON HIS FACE.

I'M TSUYU ASUI. THANK YOU FOR HAVING ME. RIBBIT RIBBIT.

BADUM
BADUM

TSUYU ASUI
↓
KANIPUSO'S AGENCY

OOPS.

WATCH OUT!

CRUNCH

HE'S A CRAB.

THE SHIP IS THE AGENCY.

OUR JOB IS TO PATROL THESE SHORES.

SEAFOOD HERO: KANIPUSO

OOPS.

I'M LATE! I'M LATE!

SQUASH

WELCOME, TSUYU!!

WHEREAS *YOU* ARE EASY TO READ, MY SHELLED FRIEND.

I MUST SAY, TSUYU, YOU HAVE QUITE THE POKER FACE.

I'M DONE... BETTER TELL HER I QUIT.

TH-THAT LADY SURE KNOWS HOW TO CRACK THE WHIP.

CREAK

WORMP

LIKE AN OPEN BOOK.

AM I THAT OBVIOUS?

HA HA HA

AN OPEN BOOK?

IT'S WRITTEN ALL OVER YOUR FACE HOW EXCITED YOU ARE TO HAVE A GIRL ON DECK.

OH YEAH... I'M READY TO BE STEPPED ON SOME MORE!

WHO ENTERS WITHOUT KNOCKING?!

GRIT

|

INCREDIBLE WORK, TSUYU!!

WE CAUGHT THE SMUGGLER!!

SMILE!!

RIBBIT.

BREATHE IN!

OH, KNOCK OFF THAT HUMBLE ACT! AT YOUR AGE, YOU SHOULD BE ACCEPTING COMPLIMENTS! BE PROUD!

RIBBIT RIBBIT

RIBBIT

ONLY BECAUSE YOU TRAINED ME SO WELL, CAPTAIN.

FWOOO

AND OUT!

RIBBIT...

HOW SHAMEFUL. I WAS ON GUARD DUTY...

HA HA HA

CHECK OUT THE AWKWARD MUG ON THIS GUY!!

I'LL DO MY BEST.

HMM, LET'S TRY LOOSENING UP THOSE FACE MUSCLES SOME MORE, TSUYU.

ACTUALLY, NO?

THAT ONE LOOKS LIKE "SAD" TO ME.

AM I REALLY THAT EXPRESSIONLESS?

LOOKS NORMAL LENGTH TO ME...

SORRY TO HEAR IT.

WELL, MY DAUGHTER'S GOT A COLD.

GLOOM

WHY THE LONG FACE, KAIZUKA?

METICULOUS JEANIST

HUH?

KATSUKI BAKUGO
↓
BEST JEANIST'S AGENCY

SLICK

TO BE HONEST, I'M NOT A FAN OF YOURS.

NO. 4 HERO: BEST JEANIST

HRM?

B·O·M·B

MY JOB AS A HERO IS REFORMING FEROCIOUS PEOPLE LIKE YOU.

SKWEEZ

SNIP

BOMB

I WAS THINKING LAYERS, MAYBE SOME HIGH-LIGHTS...

RHETORICAL QUESTION, DENIM DUDE!!

GRR

GET THOSE FREAKING SCISSORS AWAY FROM MY 'DO!! WHAT WERE YOU THINKING?!

NO. 35!!

MORE INTERN-SHIPS!!

GET THAT UNPAID EXPO-SURE!!

FRESH-SQUEEZED BAKUGO, PART 2

IT SEEMS YOU'VE LEARNED NOTHING.

PLEASE. STOP. I JUST WANNA DO HERO WORK.

A QUESTION, THEN— WHAT DOES HEROISM MEAN TO YOU?

DUNNO.

...AND BEAT THEM A HUNDRED WAYS TO HELL!!

ALL I KNOW IS, I WANNA FIND THE BAD GUYS...

NOT AGAIN !!

TRY AGAIN.

FRESH-SQUEEZED BAKUGO

ACK...

VILLAIN

BOOM

YOU'RE DEAD MEAT, YOU TWO-BIT GOON!!

?!

EEP!!

SKWEEZ

QUIRK: FIBER MASTER

HE CAN MANIPULATE CLOTHING FIBERS!! STRONG AGAINST ANYONE NOT IN THE NUDE.

C-CUT THAT OUT, ASS-HOLE!!

SQZ

SQZ

YOU MUST LEARN TEAM-WORK.

NOOOOO!!

SKWEEZ

LANGUAGE.

→ MID PUNCH INTO ZERO GRAVITY

W-WHAT'S WITH THE LOW FRAME RATE ON THIS GIRL'S MOVES? OUCH.

SLIDE

TP

↓ WEAK KICK ←←

FLOAT

FP FP

TM ZSH

↓↙← WEAK PUNCH → MID PUNCH ↑ WEAK PUNCH

ZERO GRAVITY

FWAHHH

THIS ULTIMATE MOVE TAKES A HEAVY TOLL ON THE USER.

↓↙← ↓↙← KICK KICK KICK

AMAZING, OCHACO!! THE DRAGON EVEN SHOWED UP!!

FP

23-HIT COMBO

FP

FP

FP

FP

FP

K.O.

ULTERIOR

START BY USING YOUR PHYSICAL ABILITIES AND THEN ADD YOUR QUIRK TO THE MIX.

RELYING ON YOUR QUIRK MAKES YOUR MOVES TOO SIMPLE, OKAY?

BATTLE HERO: GUNHEAD

OCHACO URARAKA & GUN-HEAD'S AGENCY

I CHOSE THIS PLACE BECAUSE OF SOME THINKING I DID AFTER THE SPORTS FESTIVAL!

YOU'RE KIND OF A BRAWLER, GUNHEAD.

BUT WHY DID YOU DRAFT ME?

...

SEE THIS, HERE?

FROM A VIDEO GAME?! The combo makes a dragon.

THERE'S A COMBO THAT I THINK WE CAN BRING TO LIFE, USING YOUR QUIRK.

FP FP

FP

32

HEROES... WE'RE HEROES...

So we're on TV now, huh.

LET'S GO ON PATROL, SHALL WE?

WHICH IS WHY I'M ABOUT TO SHOOT A COMMER-CIAL. COME AND WATCH, YOU TWO.

HEROES ALSO GET TO DO SIDE WORK.

SNAKE HERO: UWABAMI

MEDIA IS JUST ANOTHER TOOL IN A HERO'S ARSENAL.

WE BRING JOY TO MILLIONS IN AN INSTANT.

C-COMMERCIAL?

↓ UWA-BAMI'S AGENCY

MOMO YAOYO-ROZU, ITSUKA KENDO

GULP

SO HOLD THOSE HEADS A LITTLE HIGHER.

I DRAFTED YOU TWO BECAUSE I SENSED YOUR TALENT FOR SUCH THINGS.

NOT TO WORRY. I'VE SEEN THIS IN HISTORY BOOKS.

I'VE NEVER REALLY WORN MAKEUP BEFORE...

SUCH A PUSH-OVER! SHE BETTER GROW OUT OF THIS PHASE.

Thanks, girl.

With head held high!!

I'LL HAPPILY DO THE SWIMSUIT SHOOT I REFUSED TO DO EARLIER!!

THAT'S WAR PAINT!! WHY INTIMIDATE THE TV AUDIENCE?!

SHAKA

SHAKA

IT'S MEANT TO INVIGORATE ONESELF WHILE INTIMI-DATING THE ENEMY...

HERO EYE FOR THE STRAIGHT GUY

MASHIRAO OJIRO
↓
PISTOL GAY-QUARTER'S AGENCY

HUH?

AREN'T YOU A CUTIE? CAN'T WAIT TO WORK YOU OVER.

H-HE'S WASTING NO TIME!

IT GIVES A GUY IDEAS.

IDEAS?

SKWEEZ

SKWEEZ

SUCH A PLAIN FACE, BUT THIS BIG, MEATY TAIL?

EEEEK!!

C'MON, DON'T BE SO STIFF. I'LL GIVE YOU PLENTY OF TRAINING.

RUB RUB

I'M... NOT READY TO TALK ABOUT IT.

WHAT THE HECK HAPPENED TO YOU, OJIRO?!

BULGE

SOMETHING MISSING

DENKI KAMINARI
↓
ELECTO-ROCK'S AGENCY

THANK YOU.

GREAT QUIRK THERE, KID! YOU'LL GO PRO BEFORE YOU KNOW IT.

...

KINDA WORE ME OUT.

SIGH

PHEW. WHAT A WARM WELCOME.

HUH?! CALL ME BACK WHEN IT'S IMPORTANT, YOU IDIOT.

BEEP

OH...

WHAT.

JUST WONDERING WHAT YOU'RE UP TO.

...TO MY HAPPY PLACE.

BEEP BEEP

YAY

THAT TAKES ME...

STAIN

A LONER VILLAIN WHO BELIEVES THAT "HERO" IS A TITLE FOR PEOPLE WHO SAVE OTHERS, NOT THOSE WHO DON THE CAPE AND COWL TO EARN MONEY.

HE'S OVERLY OBSESSED WITH HIS PARTICULAR NOTION OF JUSTICE, AND AT SOME POINT, HE DECIDED TO GO EVANGELICAL ABOUT IT.

IF ONLY HE'D LEARNED COMPASSION FOR THOSE WITH OTHER IDEAS, HE MIGHT'VE TURNED OUT TO BE A GREAT HERO HIMSELF!!

HITOSHI SHINSO

HIS SCARY-STRONG QUIRK LETS HIM CONTROL ANYONE WHO RESPONDS TO HIM IN CONVERSATION.

HE BRAINWASHED OTHERS INTO DOING HIS BIDDING DURING THE ENTRANCE EXAM, BUT UNFORTUNATELY THE POINTS THEY EARNED DIDN'T GO TO HIM.

ALWAYS FRUSTRATED TO SEE THOSE GOOFBALLS IN CLASS 1-A MESSING AROUND LIKE CAREFREE NUMBSKULLS. DON'T GIVE UP, SHINSO!

DON'T @ ME

ALL MIGHT'S DEBUT MADE SUCH AN IMPRESSION ON HIM THAT HE DECIDED TO BECOME A HERO.

HERO KILLER STAIN. REAL NAME: CHIZOME AKAGURO.

*$0.58

...AFTER LOSING FAITH IN THE ENTIRE SYSTEM BUILT AROUND HERO EDUCATION.

I'll be rich!

I'll get chicks!

HE ATTENDED A HERO COURSE AT A PRIVATE HIGH SCHOOL BUT DROPPED OUT AFTER A FEW MONTHS...

BUT HE REALIZED THAT HIS WORDS HELD LITTLE POWER.

Heroes have become money-making tools controlled by the man! Open your eyes, sheeple!

FOR THE REST OF HIS TEEN YEARS, HE SHOUTED HIS PHILOSOPHY FROM STREET CORNERS.

...AND SPENT HIS TIME TROLLING PEOPLE ON MESSAGE BOARDS.

ENDEAVOR
@endeavor
@endeavor you think you're a ni
evil in this rotten world huh
@endeavor debate me coward
@endeavor endeavor ran away f
this debate like the coward he is
@sta-sama who the hell are you calling
a coward you faceless anon

SO HE BECAME A SHUT-IN FOR THE NEXT DECADE...

"U MAD?"

TAK TAK

NO. 36!!

THE VILLAIN WHO SMEARS HIS NAME INTO THE ANNALS OF CRIMINAL HISTORY: HERO KILLER STAIN!

I AM HERE

LEMME CHECK ALL MIGHT'S BLOG...

HERE'S HOW HIS BATTLE WITH THE KIDDIES MIGHT'VE GONE DOWN!!

BUT HE'S NOT NEARLY AS BLOOD-CURDLING IN THE WORLD OF SMASH!!

STILL NEED TO EARN THAT DOUGH

...I WILL CONTINUE MY WORK.

UNTIL THIS SOCIETY WAKES UP AND CORRECTS ITSELF...

LEAP

...

RRRING

RING

...

MANAGER FROM WORK

RRRING

STAIN... I CANNOT COMPREHEND YOUR SUFFERING.

NO. RIGHT. SORRY, I DO VALUE THIS JOB. I'LL BE RIGHT IN.

THE NIGHT SHIFT? I'M A LITTLE BUSY TONIGHT.

FAKE WOKE

TOO MANY ARE UN-DESERVING... JUST MONEY WORSHIP-PERS PLAYING HERO!

"HERO" IS A TITLE RESERVED FOR THOSE WHO PERFORM TRULY GREAT DEEDS!

I TAKE IT YOU'VE DEDICATED YOUR LIFE TO THIS CAUSE, CAREER-WISE?

YOU, UH, WANT THIS MICRO-WAVED?

LAST NIGHT, 1 A.M.

SURE.

THAT'LL BE 486 YEN.

MY APOLO-GIES.

OH YEAH, DEFINITELY... NO MORE PERSONAL QUESTIONS THOUGH.

SELF-HELP

?!

WHAM

I AM THE YOUNGER BROTHER OF A HERO YOU ATTACKED. I'VE COME TO STOP YOU.

3.19 METERS

A KID IN A COSTUME... WHO ARE YOU?

STRAIN

BUT I DON'T KNOW HOW ELSE TO DEAL WITH THESE TURBULENT EMOTIONS!!

REVENGE, THEN...? GETTING TRAPPED BY YOUR OWN HATE MAKES YOU THE FURTHEST THING FROM A HERO.

ALL MIGHT: THRILLING CLIP MONTAGE 4h56min

selected by stain

GO HOME, KID. AND WATCH THIS.

FWP

JUDGE, JURY, EXECUTIONER

...THEN CHOOSE YOUR LAST WORDS WISELY.

Native, a local hero

IF YOU'RE REALLY A HERO...

BZZT. TRY AGAIN.

YOU UGLY NOSELESS BASTARD!!

TCH.

BETTER.

I-I'VE LIVED WITHOUT REGRETS, I GUESS?

UGH...

REALLY? I'M SENSING SOME REGRET.

ONCE MORE.

LEAP

I'VE LIVED THIS LIFE OF MINE WITHOUT REGRETS!!

TANGENT

SO, THE SCENARIO WAS, THERE WAS A NUKE HIDDEN INSIDE THE VILLAIN TEAM'S HIDEOUT.

UH-HUH?

🔺 villain
♟ hero
🔻 nuke

AND THEN?

...LEARN TO WRITE MORE SPECIFIC DIRECTIONS.

TODO-ROKI!!

MIDORIYA!! WHEN CALLING FOR HELP...

ZSH

SOOO WHAT'S GOING ON HERE, EXACTLY?

HOW'D YOU LIKE TO PLAY THE PART OF IDA?

WHY ISN'T IDA PLAYING IDA?

WE'RE REENACTING OUR BATTLE TRAINING FROM VOLUME 2.

HUH ?!

PIQUED

I'M HERE TO SAVE YOU...

... IDA!

SMAASH

GIVING HELP THAT'S NOT ASKED FOR IS WHAT MAKES A *TRUE* HERO.

!

IT'S LIKE ALL MIGHT SAID.

WHY? JUST RUN.

Y-YEAH. HE TEACHES AT OUR SCHOOL.

!!

WHOA. HAVE YOU ACTUALLY MET THE BIG MAN IN THE FLESH?

UM, HE'S BAD. NOT EVEN ACCRED-ITED.

INTER-ESTING. TELL ME MORE.

WHAT'S HE LIKE AS A TEACHER?

THAT'S NO HOME RUN!!

SORRY, IDA!

COMET HOME RUN!!

HUP

NO PROBLEM.

I'M SORRY. REENACTMENT OR NOT, I CANNOT WORK ALONGSIDE THIS CRETIN.

GREAT! ANNND ACTION!

...I MIGHT'VE BEEN ONE OF THE LUCKY PROTAGS OF THIS STORY.

INCREDIBLE. IF ONLY I'D BEEN BORN A LITTLE LATER...

STOP LOOKIN' AT ME LIKE THAT, YOU DAMNED NERD!!

I WANNA WIN!! I WANNA BEAT YOU, YOU IDIOT!!

TO BE SURROUNDED BY ALL THESE GREAT SUPPORTING CHARAC- TERS...

SUCH A FUN EXERCISE... I'M JEALOUS.

...THIS BATTLE IS ABSOLUTELY NECESSARY!

FOR THE FUTURE HE STRIVES FOR...

CALL AN AMBU- LANCE... WAIT, NO, THE POLICE!!

HE'S OUT COLD...

OOPS. I ACTUALLY PUNCHED HIM.

THE FUTURE MIGHT BE IN OKAY HANDS.

Hero Killer: Defeated

DETROIT

96

SMALL WITCH ACADEMIA

SILENCE

URARAKA, Y'GOTTA HELP US OUT.

CLASSROOM SQUAD

R-REALLY?

Even Shoji's in on this?

IT'S OUR WIZARDLY FANTASY!!

MAKE US FLOAT!!

BAM

R-RIGHT, SORRY, THAT COMES FIRST.

YOU TOO, DEKU?!

WHAT ABOUT THE ACTUAL CLEANING?

DID I LEAVE SOME PRINTOUTS ON THE DESK—WHAT THE?!

YEEP!!

ACK

NO. 37!!

THE KIDS OF CLASS 1-A SURVIVED THEIR INTERNSHIPS AND MADE IT HOME ALIVE!!

BUT WHEN THEY ARRIVED BACK IN THE CLASSROOM, THEY ENCOUNTERED A THICK LAYER OF DUST AND GRIME!!

THAT'S RIGHT, THIS IS A CHAPTER ABOUT CLEANING!!

SOOT SPRITE

USE WHAT NOW?

KAMINARI, WHY DON'T YOU USE STATIC ELECTRICITY TO DO SOME DUSTING?

OH! IT'S REALLY WORKING.

FWIP

ELECTRIFICATION

KZZT

AND HAVING A BLAST!!

I'M SUCKING IT ALL UP FROM THOSE HARD-TO-REACH SPOTS!!

LEAP

ROLL-ROLL

GROSS! WHAT ATTIC WERE YOU CRAWLING AROUND IN?!

ACHOO!!

S-SORRY.

ONE-SIXTH LIFE CRISIS

WHAT'S KIRISHIMA GOT IN THIS DESK?!

HEAVY!!

KLAT

YAOYO-ROZU'S IS WEIGHTY TOO...

HE'S KEEPING DUMB-BELLS IN HERE?!

CLINK

DON'T SNOOP!

MOST OF THEM AREN'T EVEN ABOUT SELF-HELP, BUT ABOUT RELYING ON EXTERNAL, HIGHER POWERS...

PROBABLY A BUNCH OF ENCYCLOPE-DIAS... WAIT, SELF-HELP BOOKS?

HARDEN YOURSELF TO GAIA

THE LORD'S GAZE

YOUR 10 TO HEAVEN

A LOOK AHEAD

PRAISE FROM OTHER

YOU, A... YOU ARE:

P-POOR YAOYO-ROZU...

OH LORDY... SILENCE

TRUE... "ABANDON YOURSELF TO GAIA," "THE LORD'S GAZE"...

98

ROMANCE DAWN

NO CHOICE BUT TO WALK INTO THE GIRLS' BATHROOM AND BORROW THEIRS!!

WE'RE OUT OF TOILET CLEANSER!!

BOYS' BATHROOM SQUAD

I FOUND SOME MORE!

WHY DID YOU DUMP IT OUT?!

FSSH

TMP

IS THERE REALLY ANY REASON TO ENTER THE GIRLS' LAVATORY?

WHY WOULD YOU RUIN MY EXCUSE TO VENTURE INTO THAT SACRED SPACE?!

I'M TELLING SENSEI.

ARGHH!

SURE IS! EVER HEARD OF THE SPIRIT OF ADVENTURE?! EVERY MAN DREAMS OF SETTING SAIL TOWARD THAT GRAND LINE...OF STALLS!!

IT'S THE THOUGHT THAT COUNTS

GIRLS' BATHROOM SQUAD

I CAN'T GET RID OF THESE SPOTS ON THE MIRROR.

OH! LEMME TRY!

YOUR ACID? I DUNNO...

THERE'S NOTHING THIS WON'T MELT OFF!

ACID

SPLOOSH

WHY, OF COURSE I CAN CREATE A REPLACEMENT MIRROR.

STICKY SITUATION

WH-WHO DID THIS? NONE OF US EVEN CHEW GUM!!

HALLWAY SQUAD

LET ME TRY?

CRUD. IT WON'T COME OFF.

HARDENING

HMM?

OKAY. TRY AGAIN.

I'VE HEARD THAT CHEWING GUM IS EASIER TO CLEAN OFF IF YOU FREEZE IT FIRST.

HALF-COLD

THE FUTURE WOULD LOOK GRIM IF TWO OF OUR SUPER-EST POWERS COULDN'T DEFEAT GUM!!

SEE? WOW!! PEELED RIGHT OFF!

BUNCHA TOOLS

THE PLAIN BOYS

THEY DON'T NEED FIVE! AND THEY SHOULD BE USING DUST-RAGS!!

THE OTHERS STOLE ALL THE BROOMS?

STAIRS SQUAD

THIS'LL BE TOUGH WITH ONLY DUST-PANS.

THIS IS PAINSTAKING, BUT IT'LL GET THE JOB DONE.

I DUNNO ABOUT THIS...

TAPE

TAIL

WHAT A STUPEN-DOUSLY SPOTLESS STAIRCASE!!

THE STAIRS HAD NEVER BEEN CLEANER.

ADDING INSULT TO INSULT

HITOSHI SHINSO

GUY WHO WOULD SURE LIKE TO JOIN THE HERO COURSE SOMEDAY.

I SURE WOULD LIKE TO JOIN THE HERO COURSE SOMEDAY.

Am I running a kindergarten?

DRAG DRAG

HUFF. HUFF.

HOW DID THOSE WASTES OF OXYGEN STEAL MY SPOT?

WANNA HEAD TO KARAOKE, SHINSO?

1-A'S MISSING ELEMENT

Class B

SHUT UP!!

HA HA HA!

THAT HAIR! YOU'VE BEEN HOUSE-BROKEN, HAVEN'T YOU?

URK!!

BONK

KNOCK THAT OFF.

NEITO MONOMA

CLASS 1-B'S NASTY INSTIGATOR AND WASTE OF GOOD LOOKS.

ITSUKA KENDO

THE "BIG SISTER" OF CLASS 1-B!!

YOU AIN'T MY MOM! BUT YOU LOOK AS OLD AS HER!!

BOMB!!

YOU PLAY NICE TOO, BAKUGO.

AWESOME WORK! NOBODY IN OUR CLASS CAN KEEP HIM IN LINE LIKE THAT.

SORRY, I GOT CARRIED AWAY.

SUBURBIA

THE MAP SAYS IT'S AROUND HERE.

HOW'D I GET STUCK DOING THIS?

IT'S CRITICAL TO TACKLE ALL SORTS OF REAL-WORLD JOBS BEFORE YOU GO PRO!!

YOU ALSO OUGHT TO GET A GLIMPSE OF AS MANY HERO AGENCIES AS POSSIBLE, KIDS!!

REMEMBER?

HA HA HA HA

HARD TO BELIEVE ALL MIGHT'S BRANCH OFFICE IS IN THIS NEIGHBORHOOD.

"HOME SWEET A.M."?

OH, RIGHT OVER THERE!

WOMP WOMP

THAT'S JUST A NORMAL HOUSE!!

HOME SWEET A.M.

GOOFING OFF IN SHONEN JUMP!!

SPRING IS ALL ABOUT FRESH STARTS!

EVEN ALL MIGHT IS MOVING HIS AGENCY.

WE'VE BEEN ROPED INTO HELPING OUT.

*SMASH!! IS SERIALIZED IN JUMP+, BUT THIS CHAPTER RAN IN SHONEN JUMP!!

102

RETURN TO TRADITIONAL VALUES

Y-YOUR NEW OFFICE IS ON THE 23RD FLOOR OF THAT NEARBY SKYSCRAPER?!

BABAM

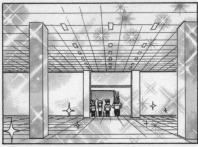

L-LISTEN, I HAD MY REASONS.

THE TAX CODE, FOR ONE...

YOU SOLD OUT TO THE BIG-CITY DEVELOPERS!!

YOU LOST SIGHT OF YOUR VALUES, DUDE!!

TRADITION

WEIRD THING FOR THESE KIDS TO GET FIRED UP ABOUT, BUT OKAY.

S-SURE.

YEAH!!

WE'RE GONNA RE-CREATE HOME SWEET A.M. HERE IN THIS SOULLESS MONUMENT TO EMPTY PROGRESS!!

HEARTWARMING

THIS *IS* JUST SOMEBODY'S HOUSE!!

TATAMI MATS? A KOTATSU TABLE?!

IT'S JUST LIKE BACK HOME...

URARAKA?!

PLIP

PLIP

I WAS LOW ON CASH, BUT I NEEDED TO EXPAND THE BUSINESS ANYWAY!!

Sorry I'm late, kids!!

FWP

HIC

THIS WAS MY BRANCH OFFICE BACK IN MY EARLY DAYS!!

ALL MIGHT WAS ONCE A STRUGGLING TWENTY-SOMETHING!

Not sure how to feel about it...

AWW

MIKAN

TOO BAD THEY'RE ABOUT TO DEMOLISH THIS PLACE FOR BEING PAST ITS TIME.

NO BONES ABOUT IT

FULL COWLING!!

ONE FOR ALL...

THIS'LL EVEN SERVE AS GOOD TRAINING!!

LEAP

PERFECT FOR QUICK, PRECISE MOVES...

SHWP

GAHHH!!

CRUNCH

ONE FOR ALL: FULL COWL-ING

THIS ISN'T A BATTLE! GO GET THAT LOOKED AT, BONE-HEAD!!

'SFINE... I'M PLENTY USED TO... BATTLING ON WITH BROKEN BONES...

STRAIN

MIDORIYA: SIDE-LINED

SUPER-STUBBED

UNDER MY SUPER-VISION.

WE CAN REALLY USE OUR QUIRKS?!

FLOAT

I'LL HANDLE THE BIG ITEMS!

QUIRK: ZERO GRAVITY

I AM THE PERFECT MAN FOR THIS JOB!!

VROOM

HEH HEH. IN THAT CASE...

GAHHH!!

QUIRK: ENGINE

WHAM

WELL YEAH, AT THAT SPEED.

YEP, TOTALLY BROKEN.

IDA: SIDE-LINED

FANBOY MODE

GET BACK TO WORK, MINETA!!

THESE TWO ARE BACK IN ACTION.

PORN! WHERE'S THE PORN?!

FWEE!!

SHF

SHF

HUH?! DON'T *EVER* COMPARE ME TO YOU!!

RIGHT?

BUT OUR QUIRKS ARE KINDA USELESS HERE.

ACK, DON'T DO THAT INSIDE!!

BESIDES, I CAN TURN THIS TRASH TO ASHES!!

EXPLO-SION

BOM

ARCHIVING PROJECTS COME LATER, MIDORIYA!!

THIS IS ALL PRECIOUS... NO WAY WE'RE THROWING IT OUT!

HMM...

FWEE

"ALL-MIGHT-RELATED BOOKS"

SPOILED ROTTEN

RIGHT, SO THE STUFF DOESN'T GO BAD.

WHILE WE'RE MOVING THE FRIDGE, YOU HANDLE THE FOOD INSIDE, TODOROKI.

HALF-COLD

KRIK

TMP

TMP

...

!

WHRRR

THESE ALL EXPIRED YEARS AGO.

HANG ON A SECOND...

VINEGAR

SOY SAUCE FOR SUSHI

MOVING JOB COMPLETE!!

AN ANIME PROPOSAL?!

"NO. 1 HERO" PROPOSAL FOR ALL MIGHT ANIME

BUT THERE'S STILL ALL THIS SPACE.

S-SUCH A FAITHFUL RE-CREATION!!

I SURE DID! THAT BRINGS BACK MEMO-RIES.

D-DID YOU WRITE THIS UP?

Y'KNOW, FOR A NATURAL OASIS IN THIS CONCRETE WASTELAND.

YOU'RE REALLY SIPPING THE TREEHUGGER JUICE, URARAKA!!

HOW ABOUT ADDING A VEGGIE GARDEN?

INSIDE?!

CAN I TAKE THIS HOME WITH ME?!

WOW, YOU'VE EVEN GOT CASTING IDEAS IN HERE.

TURNED INTO A REAL BUMPER CROP.

THEY SET UP A TOMATO GARDEN USING HYDRO-PONICS.

EXPLO-SION

THE SHREDDER

CLASSIFIED CORPO-RATE SECRETS, KID.

NOOO!!

CHILDISH GAMES

AND YOU'LL BE RUNNING AROUND THIS MOCK CITYSCAPE!!

THE TIME LIMIT IS ONE HOUR!!

KINDA ODD

EXCELLENT QUESTION!!

WHAT'S THE POINT OF PLAYING TAG?!

RUN

YOU'LL BE PROTECTING A BABY DURING THIS EXERCISE, SO TRY TO AVOID BATTLE AT ALL COSTS.

A HERO'S JOB IS SAVING PEOPLE!!

AREN'T BABIES S'POSED TO BE CUTE?!

AND BY "BABY," I MEAN THIS ROBOT!!

HUR

BL

IZUKU MIDORIYA IS A STUDENT IN U.A.'S HERO COURSE.

HIS SCHOOL HAS CLASSES THAT TRAIN STUDENTS TO BECOME HEROES!!

WHAT'S TODAY'S EXERCISE, ALL MIGHT?

YOU'RE PLAYING TAG!!

T-TAG?!

GOOFING OFF IN *SAIKYO JUMP!!*

*AND THIS CHAPTER RAN IN SAIKYO JUMP!!

107

REALISM, PART 2

...THESE ROBO-MIGHTS, BUILT BY THE SUPPORT COURSE!!

AND YOU'LL BE RUNNING AWAY FROM...

THEY'LL CHASE YOU DOWN AT THE SPEED OF A WILD RABBIT!!

THEY CAN GO 70 KILOMETERS AN HOUR!

THE HECK!! THE ROBO-MIGHTS ARE ALSO LEAKERS?!

RATTLE

SOMETHING YOU WANT TO TELL US, ALL MIGHT?!

SHWP

WE'RE GOING FOR REALISM!!

REALISM

THESE BUTT-UGLY ROBOTS, YEAH.

WE JUST NEED TO RUN AWAY WHILE CARRYING THESE ROBOTS?

HUH? WHAT NOW?!

RATTLE

ACK, MINE'S SPRUNG A LEAK!!

SPLOSH

AND NOT A TRIP TO BROWN TOWN!!

BE GLAD IT WAS JUST #1 THIS TIME!!

SHWP

WE'RE GOING FOR REALISM!!

WHY INCLUDE THAT FUNCTION?!

MATERNAL INSTINCTS

SHH!! YOU'RE GONNA GET ME CAUGHT, YOU DUMB HUNK OF JUNK!!

THERE, THERE.

WAAAH!!

MLEH, MLEH, MLEH!!

C'MON... WHO'S A GOOD ROBOT?

!

HUH?

MAMA!

MAMA!

COO COO

BADUM

SPLASH

MY CHILD AND I WILL OVERCOME WHATEVER TRIALS LIFE MAY THROW AT US!!

URARAKA UNLOCKED THE "STRONG MOTHER" CLASS.

ENDANGERMENT

59.59 REMAINING

READY? START!!

TENYA IDA

QUIRK: ENGINE

HEH!! I'M LIKE A FISH IN WATER!!

VROOM

RECIPROBURST!!

SNAP

THIS SHALL BE MY VICTORY!

FLOP

YOUR ROBOTS WON'T HOLD UP TO RECKLESS ENDANGERMENT!!

TOO LATE!

59.47 REMAINING
IDA: FAILED

M-MY BABY!!

DANGLE

HE'S GREAT WITH KIDS

SPOTTED YOU.

YIKES!! I'VE BEEN SPOTTED!!

DASH

WHOA!! KACCHAN?!

TAKE THAT!!

BoM

HOW IS YOUR BABY SURVIVING ALL THOSE VIOLENT EXPLOSIONS?

BOOM

BOOM BOOM

WHY RUN WHEN WE CAN JUST TURN 'EM TO SCRAP?!

HUH?! YOUR LITTLE GUY IS LOVING IT?!

WHEEE!!

BEAM

FOR AGES 3 AND UP

FOUND YOU.

WAH!

OH NO!

THE REAL TEST IS KEEPING OUR BABIES HAPPY.

I GET IT.

COO

GOO...

COO

THEY'RE NOT EXACTLY GOOD PLAY-THINGS FOR A ROBO-BABY.

BUT ALL I'VE GOT ON ME IS THIS SIGNED HOLOFOIL CARD AND THIS HYPER-RARE KEY CHAIN.

NOOO!!

SQUELCH

SQUISH

FOUND YOU.

GOO.

ULTIMATE MOM MOVE

NO CAUSE FOR ALARM THERE, EITHER!!

PEEK PEEK

I'LL NEVER GET CLOSE ENOUGH...

I AM HERE!!

SHNK

MORE AND MORE DISTURBING!!

A QUICK FINGER-PISTOL-UP-THE-BUTT WILL STOP A ROBO-MIGHT IN ITS TRACKS!! BUT YOU GOTTA KEEP THOSE FINGERS UP THERE!

URARAKA DIDN'T HESITATE FOR A SECOND?!

TAKE THIS!!

SHNK

...IS A SMALL PRICE TO PAY.

THE FIRE IN THOSE EYES! INTENSE!!

MY CHILD'S LIFE IS ON THE LINE, SO ROBO BUTT...

GOT MILK?

THE BABIES YOU'RE CARRYING...

44:57 REMAINING

UP IT? HOW?

LET'S UP THE CHALLENGE A BIT!!

THAT'S JUST DISTURBING!!

GOO GOO...

GAUNT

...WILL "DIE" IF THEY'RE NOT BREASTFED!!

NO CAUSE FOR ALARM!!

BREASTFED? BUT HOW...?

EVEN MORE DISTURBING!!

LEAK

FOR THE ROBO-MIGHTS WILL START LACTATING WHEN THEY SPOT A BABY!!

SMASHING BOUNDARIES

I AM H-URK!!

WH WH

DET ROIT

SMASH

AM

I CAN'T BELIEVE I HAVE TO DO THIS TO MY IDOL! UGH!!

NOW, KACCHAN!! PLEASE!!

P.LRK

I CAN'T BELIEVE I HAVE TO TEAM UP WITH DEKU! UGH!!

GAH... SCREW THIS!!

DESPERATE TIMES CALL FOR DESPERATE MEASURES.

ARGH HHH!!

A MATTER OF HANDS

Y-YOU TOO, ASUI?!

ANY-THING FOR THE MISSION.

FREEZE

I AM HERE!!

OH? IT REALLY STOPPED HIM.

SHNK

WHAT A SCENE.

HMPH!

SUCK SUCK

THERE YOU GO, LITTLE ONE.

EVERY-ONE'S SOME-HOW ON BOARD WITH THIS?!

SHNNNNK

TEAM UP WITH ME, KACCHAN?

IN YOUR DREAMS !!

B-BUT HOW DO I PULL OFF THE FINGER-PISTOL AND HOLD MY BABY SIMULTANE-OUSLY?

POST-ROBO DEPRESSION

YOU MUST BE COLD, OCHA-ZUKE? JUST HANG IN THERE...

HEH HEH.

YES, I SUPPOSE IT'S MEAL-TIME.

WHAT'S THAT? YOU'RE HUNGRY?

HEH HEH ...

HAVING TO RETURN THE ROBO BABY DID A NUMBER ON URARAKA.

WHY IS SHE SPEAKING TO THAT EMPTY STROLLER?

IT TOOK A GOOD SIX MONTHS FOR OCHACO'S PSYCHE TO STABILIZE.

NOOO! OCHA-ZUKE!!

PRECIOUS MOMENTS

FLBBBT I SMELL A #2!!

THEY ENDURED ALL MANNER OF "MISSIONS" THROUGH-OUT THE EXERCISE.

POOP

15:08 REMAINING

Baby name → OH, OCHA-ZUKE ...

07:56 REMAINING

I'LL NEVER LEAVE YOU.

...

SKWEEN

MAMA.

03:11 REMAINING

AGAIN?! RIGHT IN THE FINAL STRETCH?

FLBBBT

YET THEY EMERGED TRIUM-PHANT.

POOP

00:00 REMAINING

...THEY EMERGED HARDENED TO THE CHALLENGES OF THIS WORLD.

AND AFTER THAT SINGLE HOUR OF TRAIN-ING...

TRAINING COMPLETE!!

VOLUME 2 - END

VOLUME 2'S GOT A BUTTLOAD OF BONUS CONTENT TOO!!

PERUSE AT YOUR OWN PACE!!

←~ Author

BONUS STUFF!!

AHHH!! YOU GUYS!!

WIDDLE

GLAD YOU'RE HERE, MIDORIYA. HANDLE THEM, WOULD YOU?

IS THAT REALLY YOU, KACCHAN?

So itty-bitty

FWEEE

MY ERASURE IS KEEPING HIM IN CHECK, BUT I CAN'T LET HIM OUT OF MY SIGHT.

HUH?

THIS VILLAIN DE-AGES PEOPLE BY DOING THAT FINGER WHISTLE.

COOL STUFF. WHAT'S THE SCIENCE BEHIND THIS...?

EH?

BOOP

TAKE CARE OF THE OTHERS UNTIL BACKUP ARRIVES.

A VILLAIN WITH A PARTICULARLY TERRIFYING QUIRK CAME TO TOWN ONE DAY!!

THE 1-A KIDS HAPPENED TO ENCOUNTER THIS VILLAIN, AND THEY PAID THE PRICE.

ONLY DEKU ESCAPED UNSCATHED!! HOW WILL HE NAVIGATE THIS WACKY SCENARIO?!

TERRIBLE FOURS

Y-YOU'VE GOT A TAIL, ASUI!!

HMM?

POKE

SORRY.

TOO CUTE.

AWW

I HATE IT. I WANNA DO METAMOR-PHOSIS.

FROG

AND OJIRO'S TAIL IS STILL TINY?

POKE

NAW, THAT AIN'T RIGHT! WE'RE HUMANS!!

PEEP.*

WAIT. FOR REAL?

BAM

*TRANSLATION: BEHOLD, THE ABYSS.

DEKU DAY CARE

SOOO YOU GUYS REMEMBER WHO I AM?

TAKE CARE OF THEM? WHAT'S THAT EVEN MEAN?

W-WHAT?! I'M ONLY 15!!

THEIR MEMORIES REVERTED TOO?

SHOCK

OLD MAN.

GET BACK HERE, AOYAMA!! THAT'S DANGER-OUS!!

ZSH

TMP. TMP.

ONE OF THEM'S HEADED FOR TRAFFIC, MIDORIYA!!

THIS IS MY MOST DAUNTING MISSION YET!!

ACK!! YOU SIT STILL TOO, KACCHAN!!

TODDLE

PRODIGY'S LAMENT

ARRESTED DEVELOPMENT

LI'L SHOTA

DRY EYE →

SHAKA SHAKA

UGH. WHAT'S TAKING THOSE OTHER HEROES SO LONG?

THAT'S HOW IT WORKS!

I SEE. HE CAN ONLY ERASE MY QUIRK AS LONG AS HE DOESN'T BLINK.

ORIN

OH NO!!

ROAR

PUFF PUFF

STOP BLOWING INTO MY EYES!!

WHAT'S WITH THE BOWL CUT? YIKES!!

POOF

GAH! AIZAWA SENSEI!!!

...

ROLE-REVERSAL

WHAP

AH.

EAT THIS, OLD MAN!!

BOM

OWWIE.

BONK

ACK.

YOU OKAY, LI'L KACCHAN?!

FWP

OH NO!! I PUT TOO MUCH FORCE INTO THAT!!

YOU'RE REALLY, REALLY STRONG.

TEACH ME THAT MOVE.

FIDGET

HUH?

YOU BET, KID!!

SKWEEZ

I WANNA BE LIKE YOU WHEN I GROW UP.

HOW'S HE THE CUTEST ONE OF ALL?!

118

LI'L KACCHAN AND ME

SO THAT QUIRK ACTIVATES WHEN HE WHISTLES, RIGHT?

I'M THE ONLY ONE LEFT. THEY'RE COUNTING ON ME!!

I'VE GOT AN IDEA THAT JUST MIGHT WORK!!

HEH HEH

BREATHE

FOLLOW ME, KIDDIES! WE'LL ALL GO LIVE IN A CAVE TOGETHER!!

HUH... BUT...

BAM

KAC-CHAN!! BLOW UP MY EARS!!

GRP

DON'T WORRY, CUZ...

...I'M GONNA SAVE YOU.

BACKFIRE

WHO'S MAKING MISCHIEF IN OUR TOWN?

BAM

YOU TWO!!

Finally.

LET'S GET THIS OVER WITH. I NEED TO USE THE BATHROOM.

THE NEW, SMALLER BLADDER CAN'T BE HELPING!!

POOF

PEE-PEE, PEE-PEE.

TRY TO HOLD IT IN, SENSEI!!

I GOTTA GO!

YOU'RE THE ONE MAKING MISCHIEF NOW!!

FLIP

OOH HOO.

TOO MANY RUG RATS...

GAB

GAB

UGHH...

YAP YAP

SAPPY EPILOGUE

THE EFFECTS OF THE VILLAIN'S QUIRK WERE ONLY TEMPORARY, SO THEY STARTED AGING BACK, GETTING ONE YEAR OLDER EVERY DAY.

AFTER THAT, EVERYONE GOT THE DIAPER CHANGES THEY NEEDED.

ARGH!!

BOOOM

FWEEEE

OH! MORNING, KACCHAN!

DASH

YIKES! I'M GONNA BE LATE!!

HUM

MMM

THEY LOST THEIR MEMORIES OF THAT DAY, BUT SOMETHING MUST'VE STUCK, SINCE KACCHAN SEEMED TO BE A LITTLE NICER TO ME.

LATE? YEAH, CUZ OF THAT BIG GOOFY BACKPACK YOU LOVE.

WAH.

GIVE IT HERE.

FWIP

YOU SAVED THE DAY.

YOU DID IT.

HEH. HIS QUIRK DIDN'T AFFECT ME.

DID I SAY NICER? NEVER MIND.

THIS'LL GET IT TO SCHOOL FASTER.

BOOM

VOOOSH

WAIT... NO. WHAT'RE YOU DOING?!

SMASH!!

DETROIT

The assignment this time was de-aged designs. I didn't think too hard about this and just had fun drawing them.

MY HERO KINDERGARTEN

SMASH!! VOLUME 2

KOHEI HORIKOSHI

I haven't shown up yet.

BEHIND THE SCENES

When *Smash!!* was still in the planning phase, I told Neda, "Don't poke too much fun at the villains." Villains are supposed to be unsettling and terrifying, right? So I wanted *Smash!!* to respect that.

But once the series started rolling and I began to get a taste for the world Neda was creating, I realized I was wrong. It was a different series, drawn by him, and any arbitrary restrictions I put in place would only limit the scope of what he could do with it. I ended up telling him, "Actually, go nuts with the villains."

Sorry about the flip-flopping, Neda!!

Poke as much fun as you want, because I'm looking forward to it!!

CAST OF CHARACTERS

NEDA
AUTHOR OF *SMASH!!* CONSTANTLY RUDE TO EDITORS. PLENTY TO BE CONCERNED ABOUT WITH THIS GUY.

HATTORI
NEDA'S EDITOR WHEN THIS STORY TOOK PLACE. APPEARS AS HIMSELF IN *BAKUMAN*. A PAIN IN THE BUTT WHEN HE'S DRUNK.

YASUKI TANAKA
GURU TO BOTH NEDA AND HORIKOSHI. GIVES THEM GUIDANCE WITH THE GENEROSITY AND FORBEARANCE OF THE BUDDHA.

HORIKOSHI
AUTHOR OF *MY HERO ACADEMIA*. THIS DUKE OF SLEEPY TIME LOVES SLEEPING MORE THAN LITERALLY ANYTHING ELSE IN THE WHOLE WIDE WORLD.

HORIKOSHI AND ME

CHAPTER 2: THE REUNION

THIS TAKES PLACE ONE YEAR AFTER CHAPTER 1 OF "HORIKOSHI AND ME." THEY HAD BEEN DUMB ENOUGH TO GIVE ME THE NEWCOMER'S PRIZE THE FOLLOWING YEAR, BUT THEN I FOUND MYSELF AT A CREATIVE DEAD END.

I'M NOT IMPROVING AT ALL. WHAT THE HECK DO I DO?

HRM...

YOU WANT TO WORK AS AN ASSISTANT?

HUH?

HATTORI

THE MARS VOLTA

BAM

SHUEISHA

JUMP IS TAKING SUBMISSIONS. WHY NOT SEND US A FEW PAGES?

WELL, YOUR ART STYLE SURE IS, UH, UNIQUE...

HMM

S-SURE.

SO MAYBE IT'D HELP TO SEE HOW A PRO RUNS THEIR OPERATION?

HMM.

I'M JUST NOT GETTING ANY BETTER ON MY OWN.

I'M TOO SOFT FOR THIS HARSH WORLD.

WINNING THAT PRIZE DIDN'T DO SQUAT FOR ME.

GUESS I JUST GOTTA KEEP DRAWING.

TWO YEARS LATER

"ME"?

HE SOUNDS LIKE THE GUY WITH THAT NINJA NAME...

HELLO? IT'S ME.

MY PHONE HASN'T RUNG IN EXACTLY TWO YEARS!!

RRRING

JOLT

SERI-OUSLY, HANZO?!

AGAIN, IT'S HATTORI.

ALSO, YOU MENTIONED WANTING ASSISTANT WORK, RIGHT? STILL UP FOR THAT...?

SERIOUSLY, HANZO?!

BADUM

UM, THE NAME'S HATTORI.

WE'RE GOING TO RUN THOSE PAGES YOU SENT IN WAY BACK WHEN.

124

IN CLOSING

THANK YOU FOR CHOOSING TO PURCHASE *MY HERO ACADEMIA: SMASH!!* VOLUME 2 FOR SOME REASON.

TO THE READERS WHO SPEND MONEY ON THIS UNWORTHY POOP, TO HORIKOSHI WHO FORGIVES MY EVERY INDISCRETION, TO MY SUPPORTIVE FAMILY, FRIENDS AND EDITORS... I'M SO GRATEFUL TO ALL OF YOU I WISH I COULD BOW DOWN AT YOUR FEET, GRINDING MY HEAD INTO THE DIRT.

I WORK HARD IN THE HOPES THAT SOMEBODY, ANYBODY OUT THERE MIGHT THINK, "THIS WAS A WORTHWHILE PURCHASE" OR "WELL, IT WASN'T THE WORST MANGA I'VE EVER READ, I GUESS?" SO PLEASE KEEP THAT IN MIND, GOING FORWARD.

SEE YOU IN VOLUME 3.

根田 啓史

HIROFUMI NEDA

MT. LADY ON AN AVERAGE WEEKNIGHT

Big Potato

MY HERO ACADEMIA

SCHOOL BRIEFS

ORIGINAL STORY BY
KOHEI HORIKOSHI

WRITTEN BY
ANRI YOSHI

Prose short stories featuring the everyday school lives of My Hero Academia's fan-favorite characters!

VIZ

Dr.STONE

STORY BY
RIICHIRO INAGAKI

ART BY
BOICHI

One fateful day, all of humanity turned to stone. Many millennia later, Taiju frees himself from petrification and finds himself surrounded by statues. The situation looks grim—until he runs into his science-loving friend Senku! Together they plan to restart civilization with the power of science!

DEMON SLAYER
KIMETSU NO YAIBA

Story and Art by
KOYOHARU GOTOUGE

In Taisho-era Japan, kindhearted Tanjiro Kamado makes a living selling charcoal. But his peaceful life is shattered when a demon slaughters his entire family. His little sister Nezuko is the only survivor, but she has been transformed into a demon herself! Tanjiro sets out on a dangerous journey to find a way to return his sister to normal and destroy the demon who ruined his life.

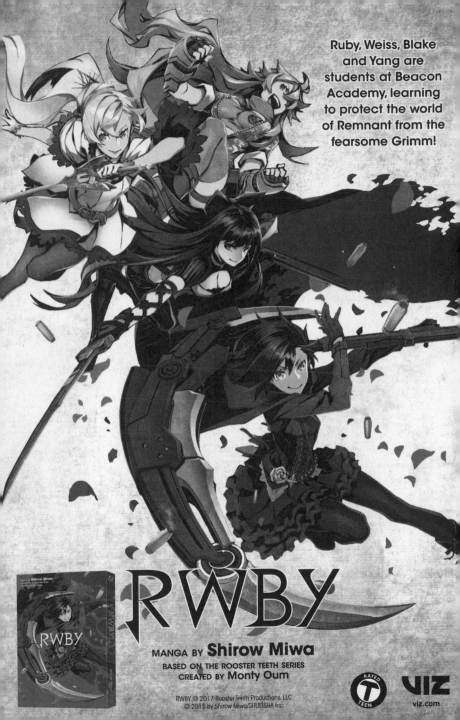

Ruby, Weiss, Blake and Yang are students at Beacon Academy, learning to protect the world of Remnant from the fearsome Grimm!

RWBY

MANGA BY **Shirow Miwa**

BASED ON THE ROOSTER TEETH SERIES
CREATED BY **Monty Oum**

RATED TEEN

VIZ
viz.com